IMMORTAL HYMNS

— PIANO LEVEL —
EARLY INTERMEDIATE
(HLSPL LEVEL 4-5)

ISBN 978-0-634-03632-3

HAL•LEONARD®
CORPORATION

7777 W. BLUEMOUND RD. P.O. BOX 13819 MILWAUKEE, WI 53213

Visit Hal Leonard Online at
www.halleonard.com

PREFACE

It was a real joy to arrange this collection for you. Deciding which hymns to include presented a challenge, however. There are so many classics! These seventeen titles represent a wide stylistic range—from majestic ("All Hail the Power of Jesus' Name") to serene ("Softly and Tenderly"). Although arranged to stand alone as piano solos, lyrics have been included with each piece to help inform your instrumental interpretations.

New praise and worship songs are written every year. These compositions bring a contemporary voice to our expressions of faith, both in musical and lyrical style. I am often inspired and deeply moved by these new songs. But I can never imagine losing touch with the bedrock hymns that have been with us for generations. These melodies and texts are timeless. They are the very definition of "evergreen."

I hope this collection of immortal hymns will inspire you and those who hear them for years to come!

Sincerely,
Phillip Keveren

◆

BIOGRAPHY

Phillip Keveren, a multi-talented keyboard artist and composer, has composed original works in a variety of genres from piano solo to symphonic orchestra. Mr. Keveren gives frequent concerts and workshops for teachers and their students in the United States, Canada, Europe, and Asia. Mr. Keveren holds a B.M. in composition from California State University Northridge and a M.M. in composition from the University of Southern California.

CONTENTS

ALL HAIL THE POWER OF JESUS' NAME

Words by EDWARD PERRONET
Altered by JOHN RIPPON
Music by JAMES ELLOR
Arranged by Phillip Keveren

With strength

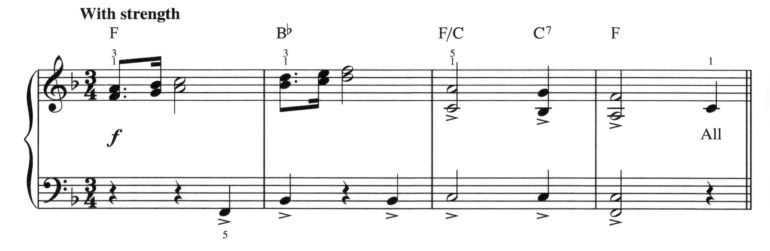

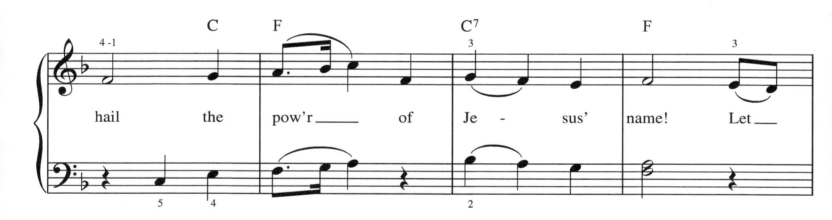

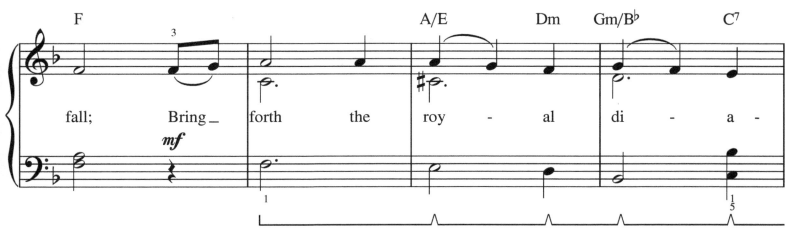

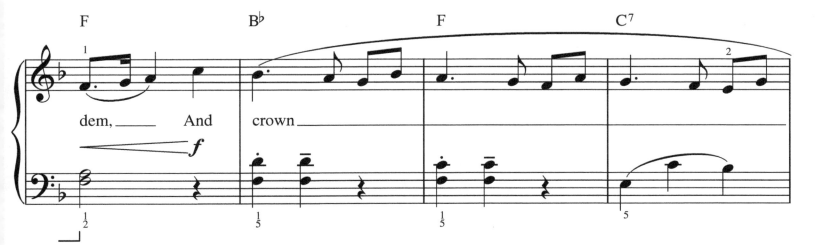

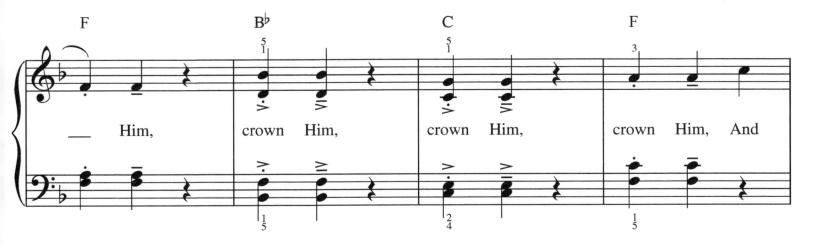

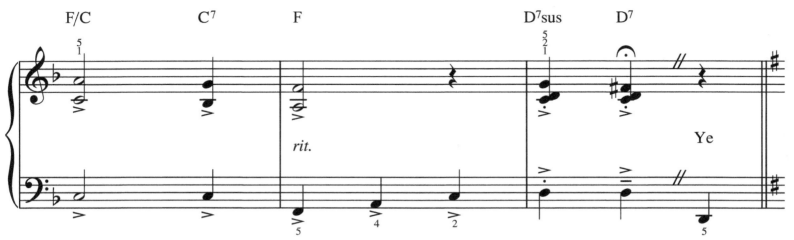

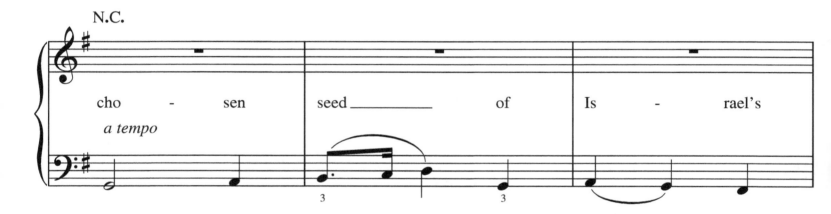

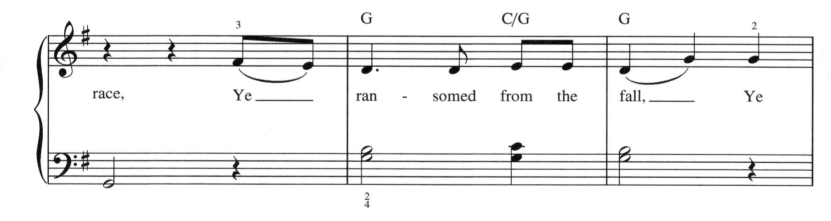

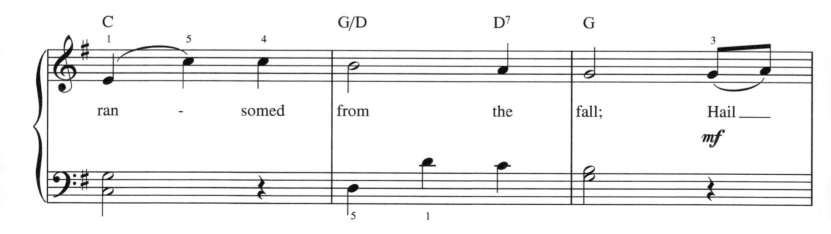

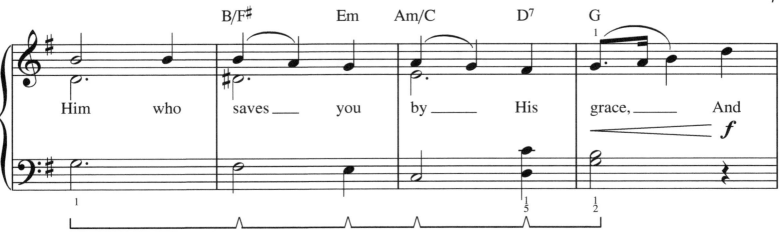

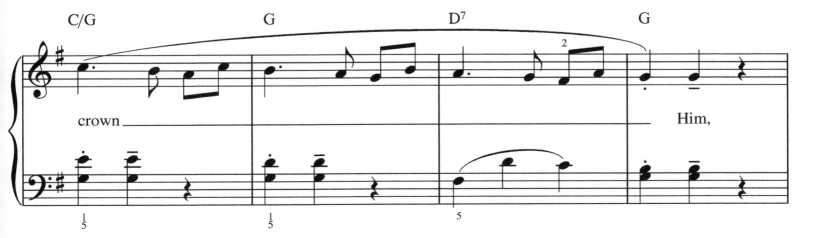

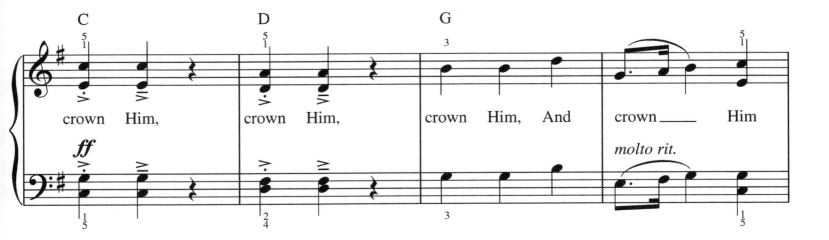

AND CAN IT BE
THAT I SHOULD GAIN

Words by CHARLES WESLEY
Music by THOMAS CAMPBELL
Arranged by Phillip Keveren

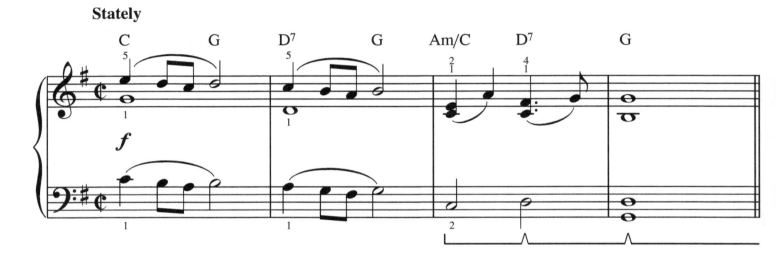

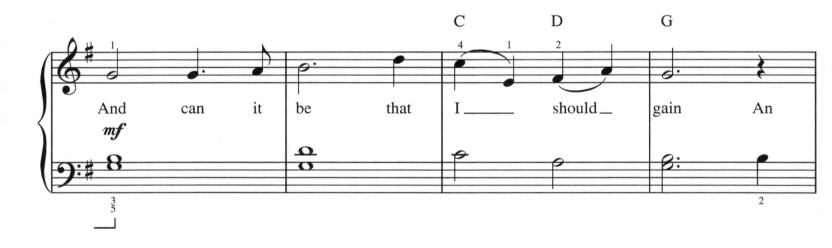

And can it be that I _____ should __ gain An

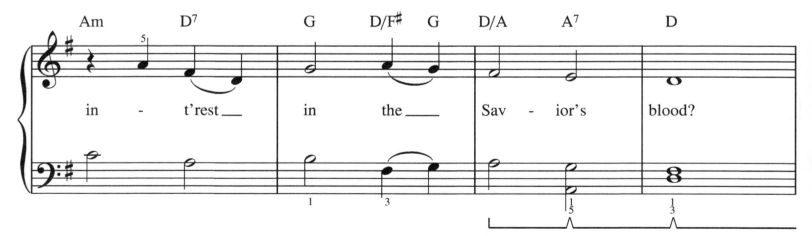

in - t'rest ____ in the ____ Sav - ior's blood?

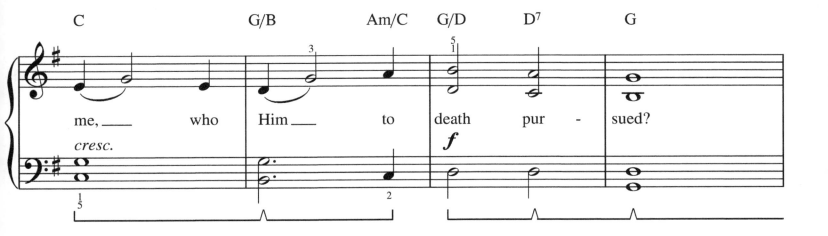

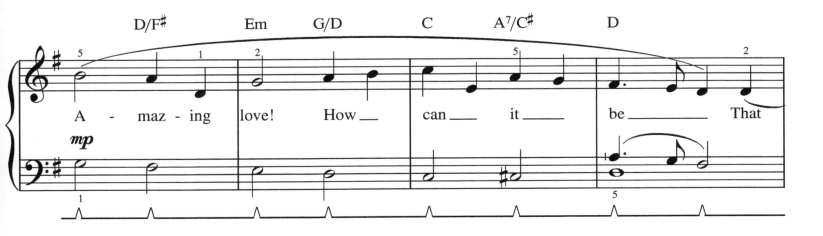

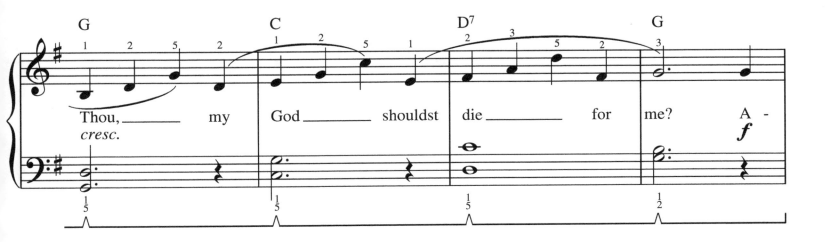

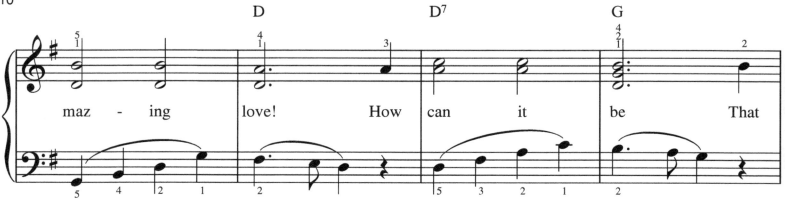

maz - ing love! How can it be That

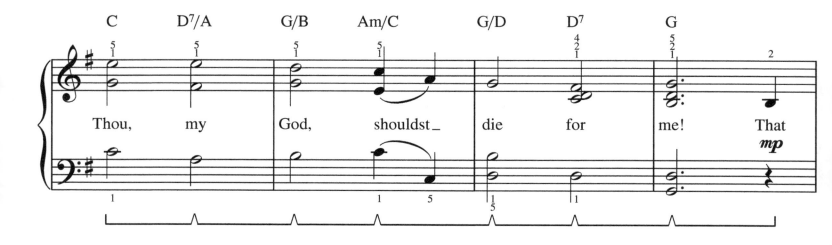

Thou, my God, shouldst _ die for me! That

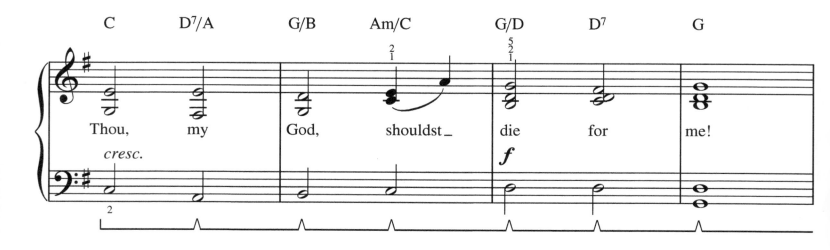

Thou, my God, shouldst _ die for me!

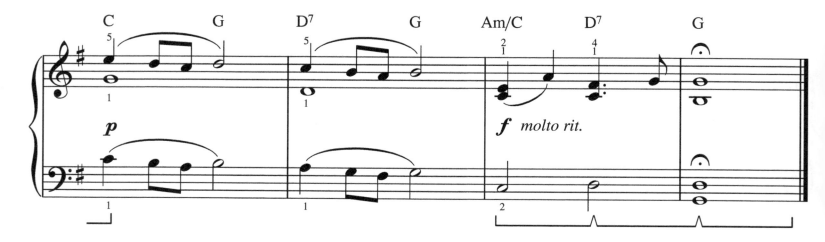

BE THOU MY VISION

Traditional Irish
Translated by MARY E. BYRNE
Arranged by Phillip Keveren

Slowly, expressively

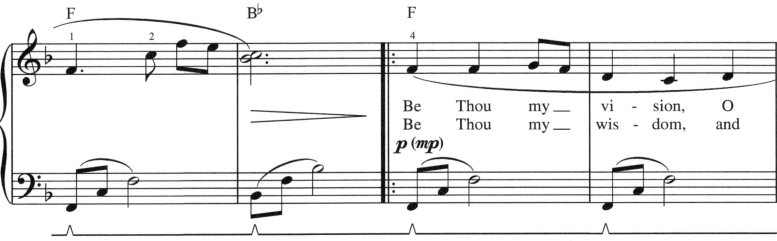

Be Thou my __ vi - sion, O
Be Thou my __ wis - dom, and

Lord of my heart;
Thou my true Word;

Naught be all else to me
I ev - er with Thee and

save that Thou art;
Thou with me, Lord;

Thou my __ best __ thought, __ by
Thou my __ great __ Fa - ther,

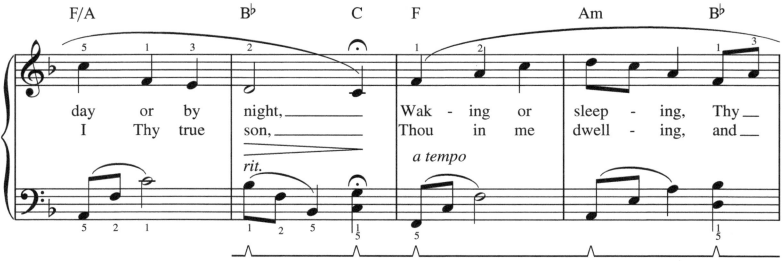

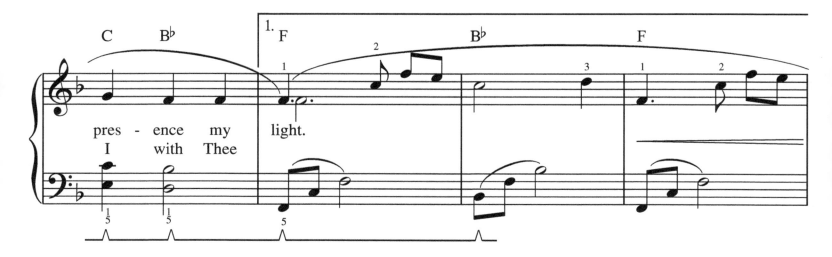

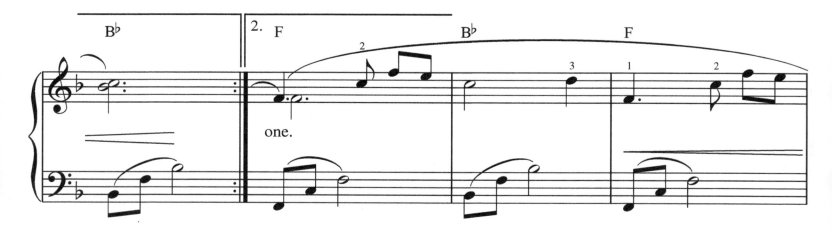

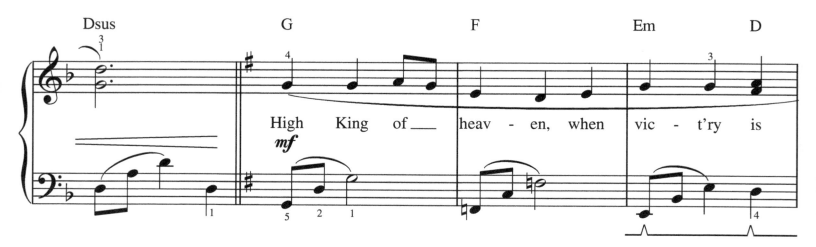

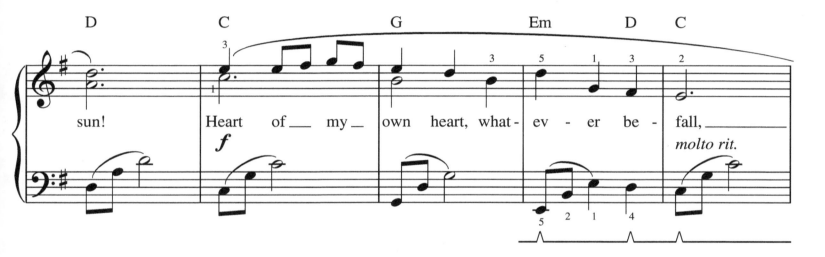

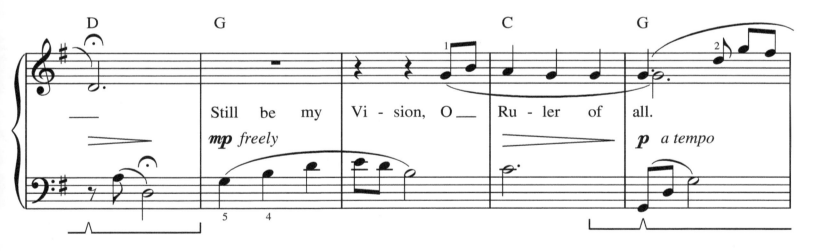

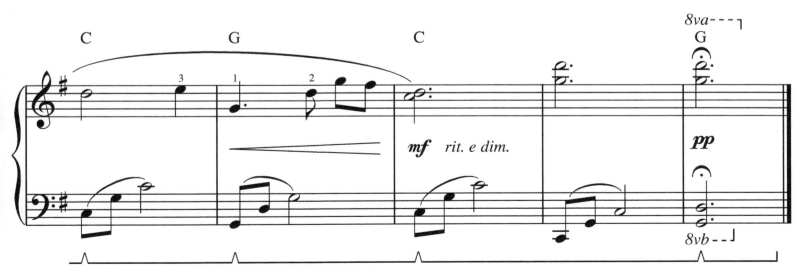

CHRIST THE LORD IS RISEN TODAY

Words by CHARLES WESLEY
Music Adapted From *Lyra Davidica*
Arranged by Phillip Keveren

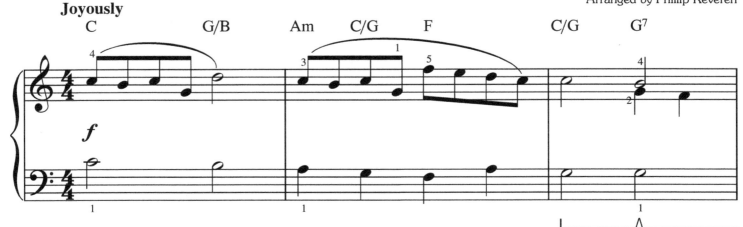

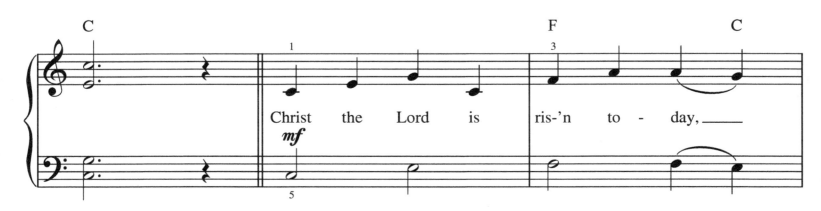

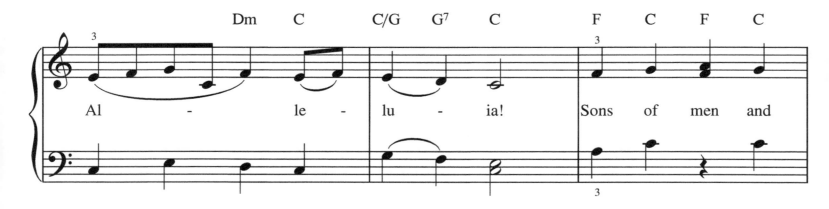

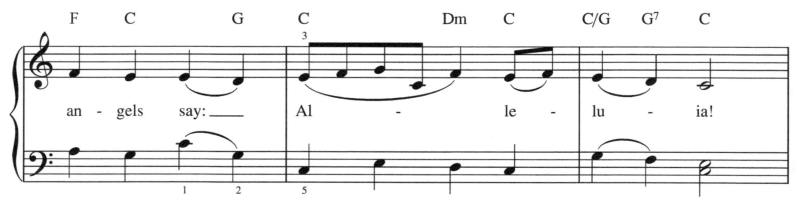

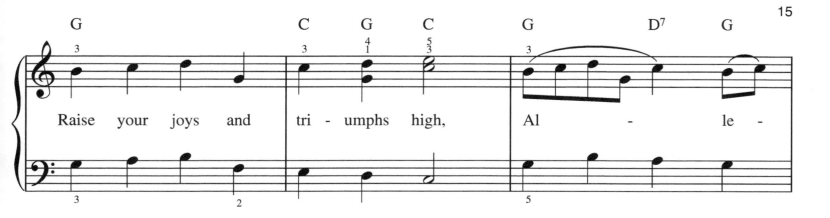

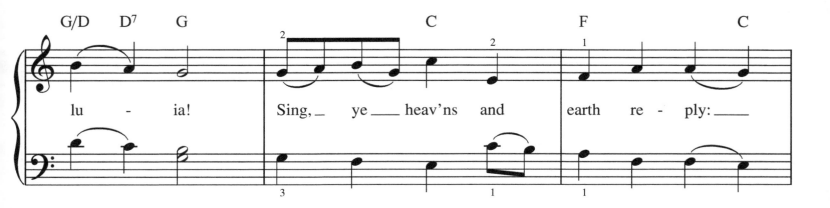

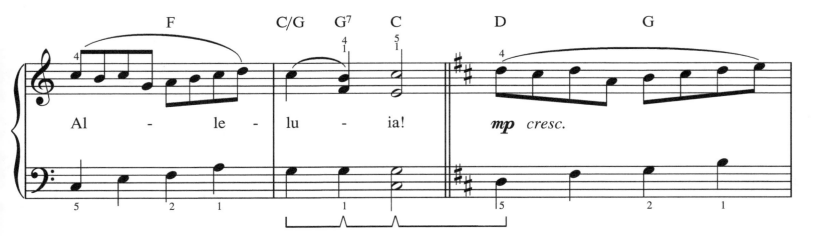

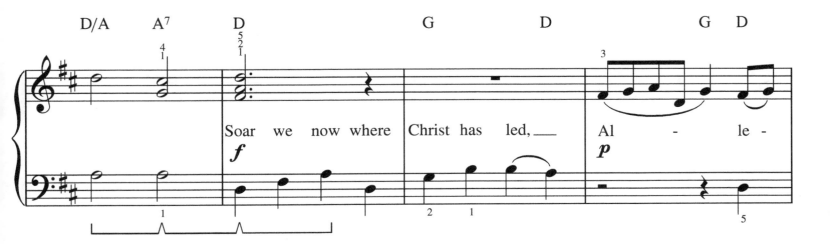

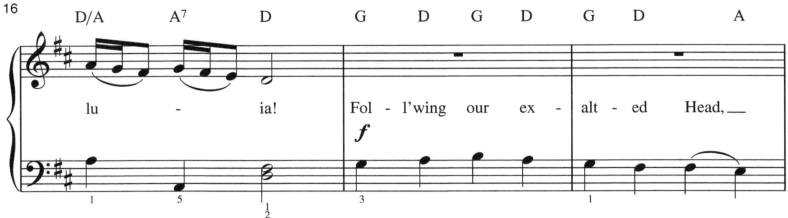

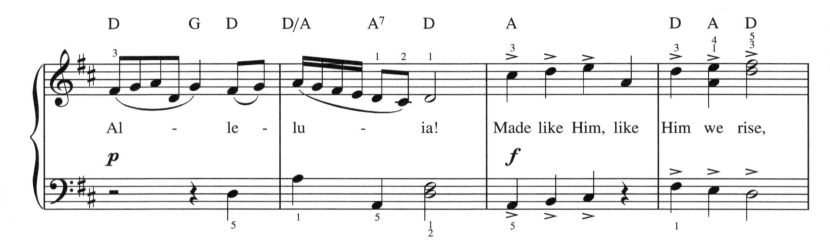

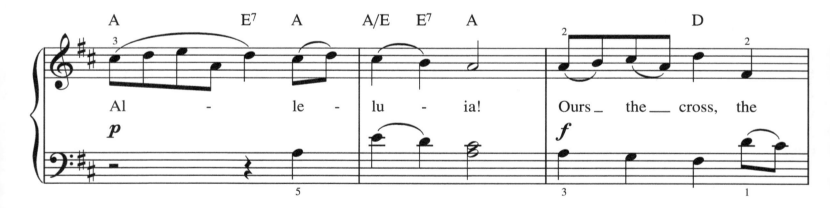

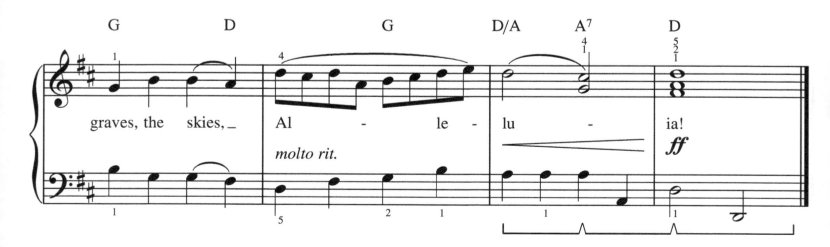

COME, THOU ALMIGHTY KING

Traditional
Music by FELICE DE GIARDINI
Arranged by Phillip Keveren

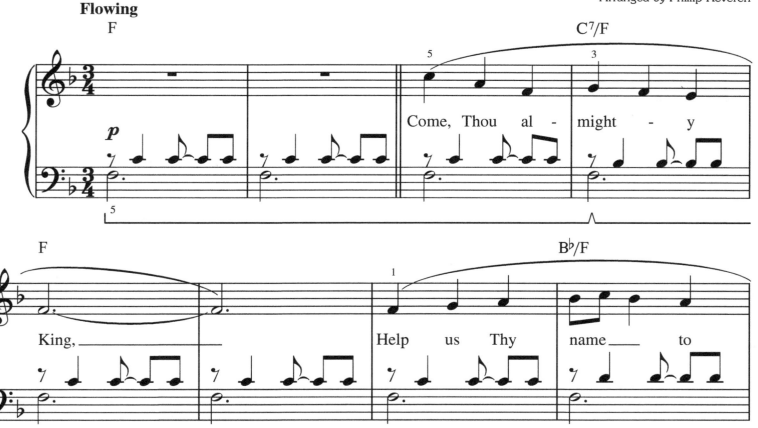

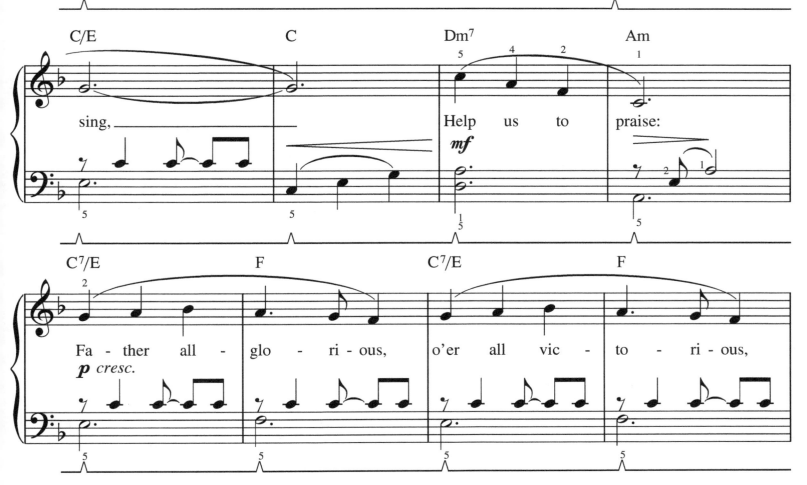

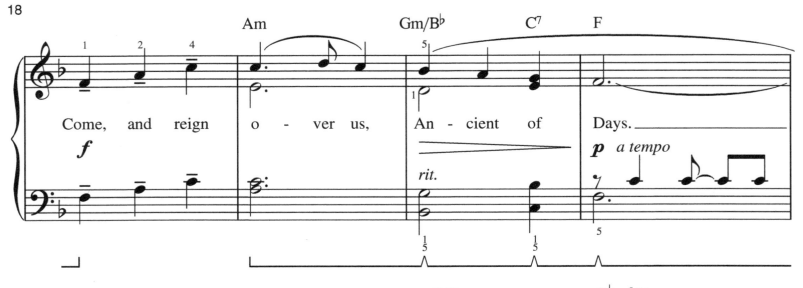

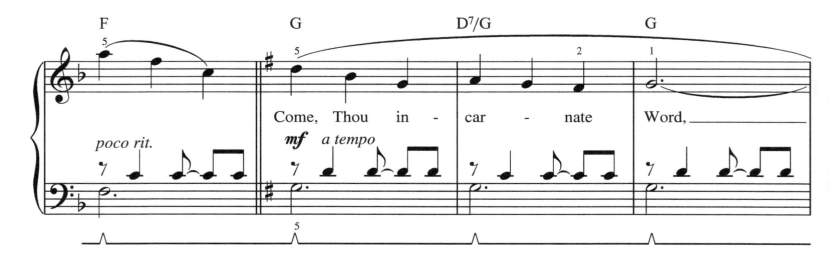

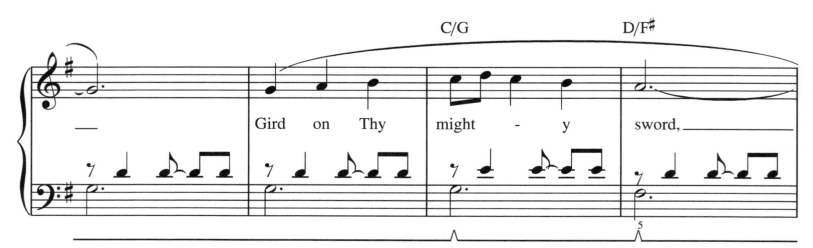

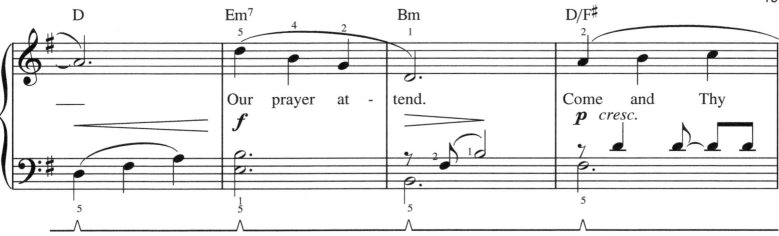

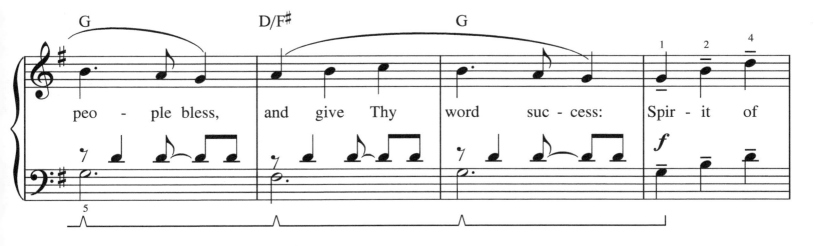

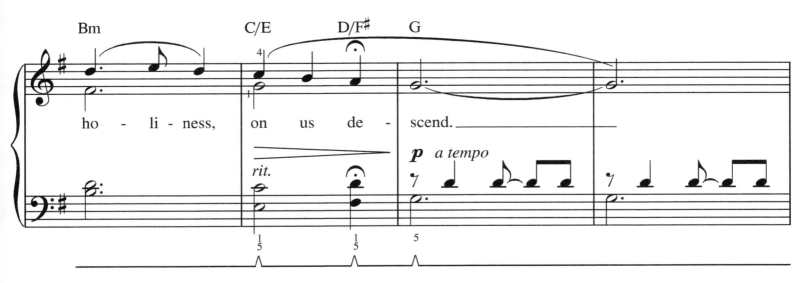

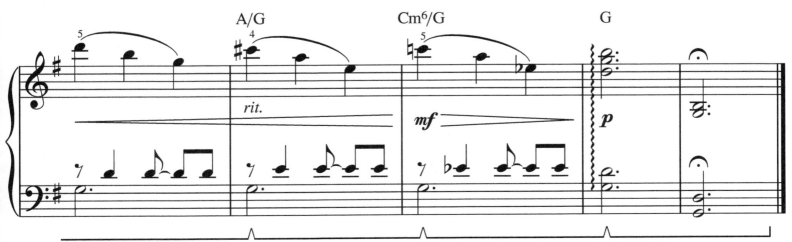

COME, THOU FOUNT OF EVERY BLESSING

Words by ROBERT ROBINSON
Music from John Wyeth's *Repository of Sacred Music*
Arranged by Phillip Keveren

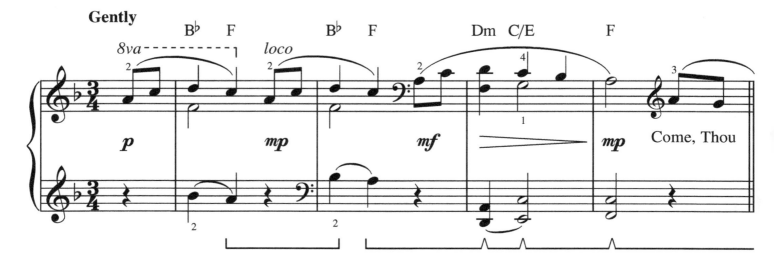

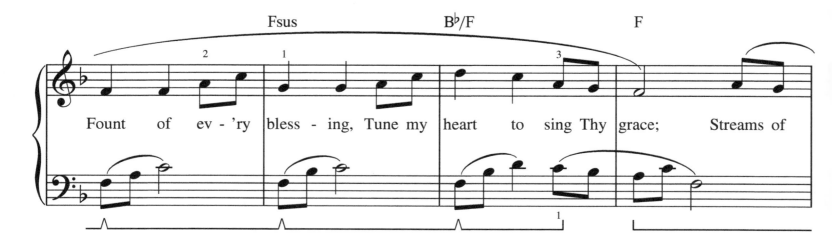

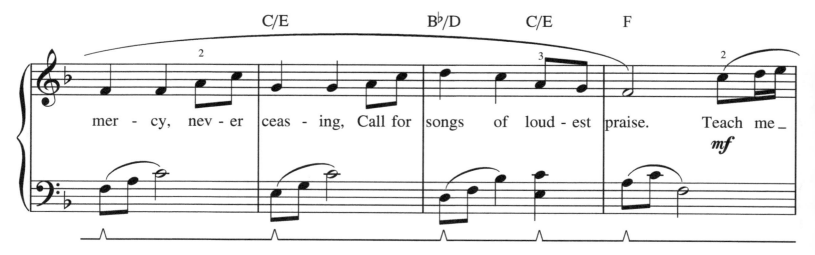

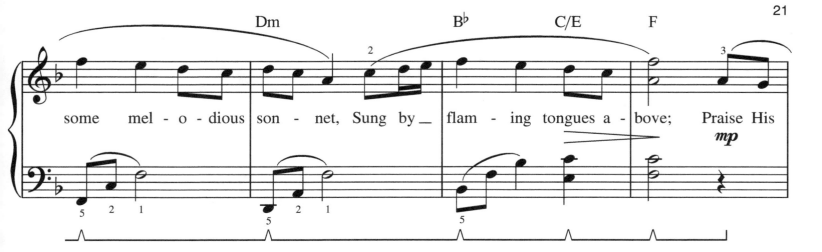

some mel - o - dious son - net, Sung by __ flam - ing tongues a - bove; Praise His

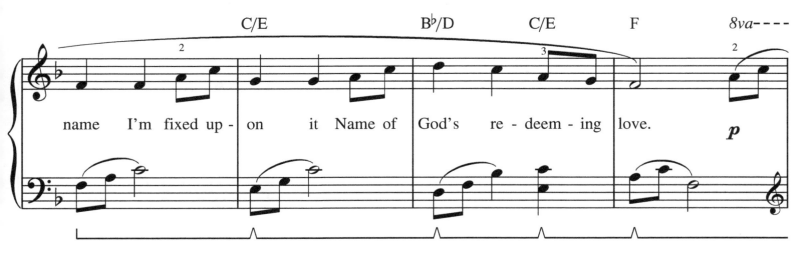

name I'm fixed up - on it Name of God's re - deem - ing love.

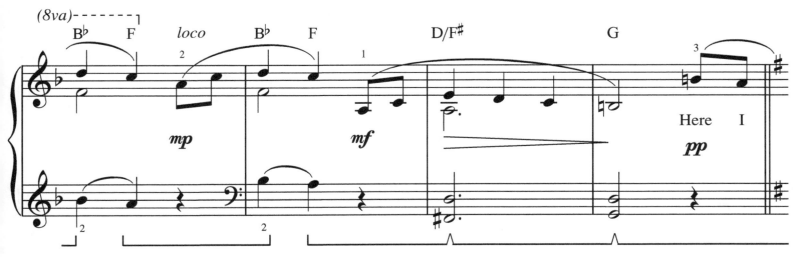

raise mine Eb - e - ne - zer; Hith - er by Thy help I'm come; And I

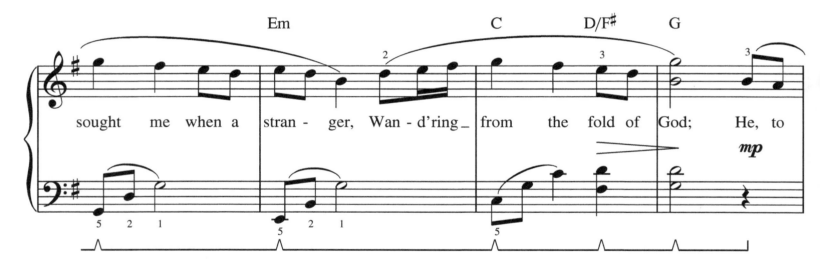

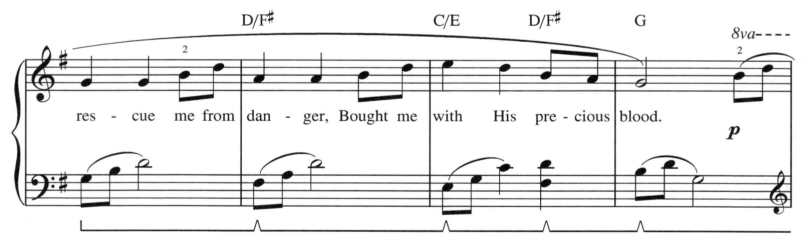

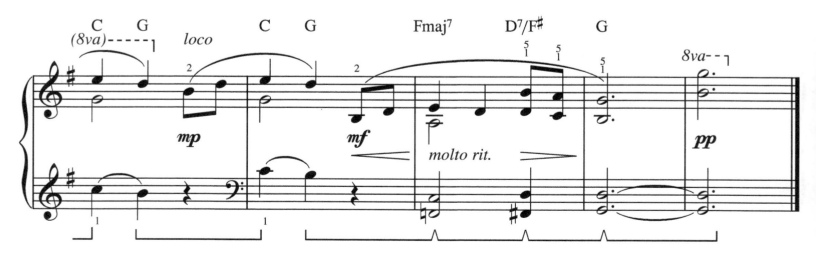

GOD OF OUR FATHERS

Words by DANIEL CRANE ROBERTS
Music by GEORGE WILLIAM WARREN
Arranged by Phillip Keveren

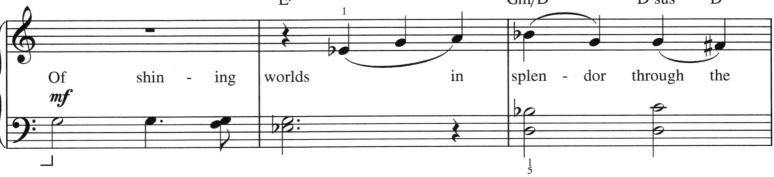

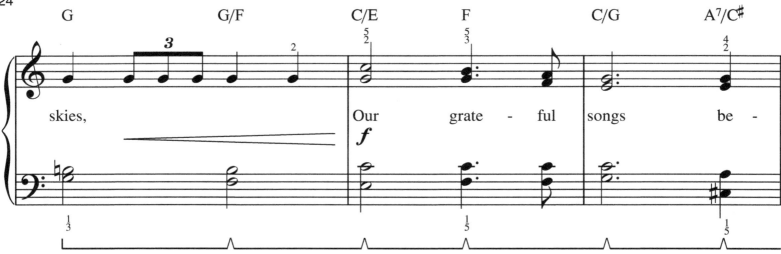

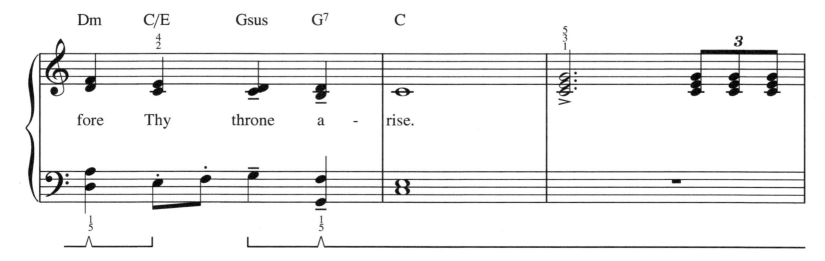

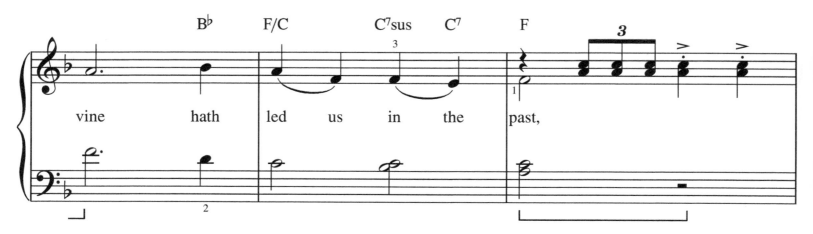

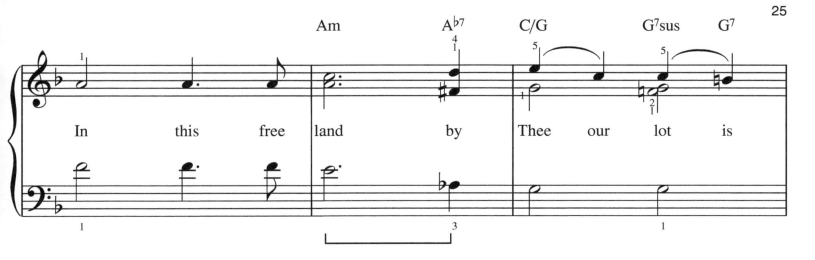

In this free land by Thee our lot is

cast; Be Thou our Rul - er,

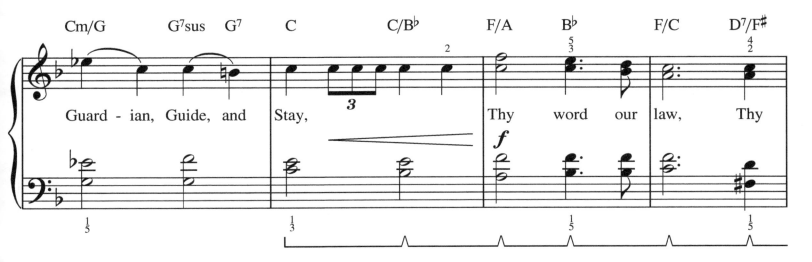

Guard - ian, Guide, and Stay, Thy word our law, Thy

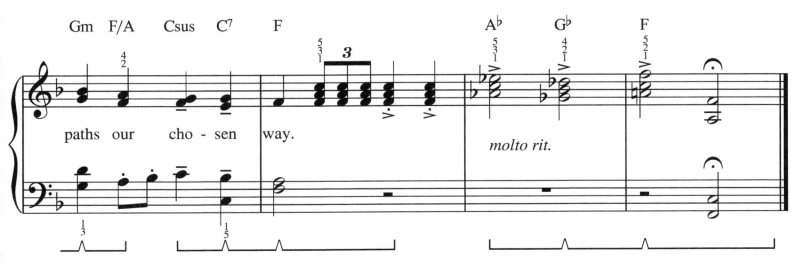

paths our cho - sen way.

HOLY, HOLY, HOLY

Text by REGINALD HEBER
Music by JOHN B. DYKES
Arranged by Phillip Keveren

With reverence

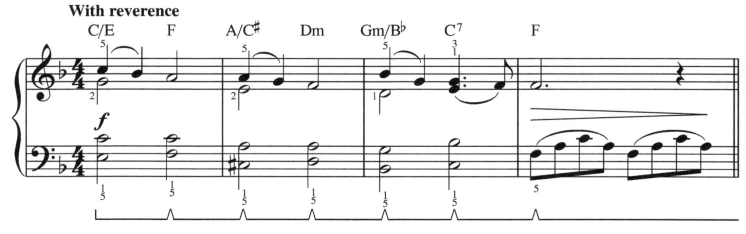

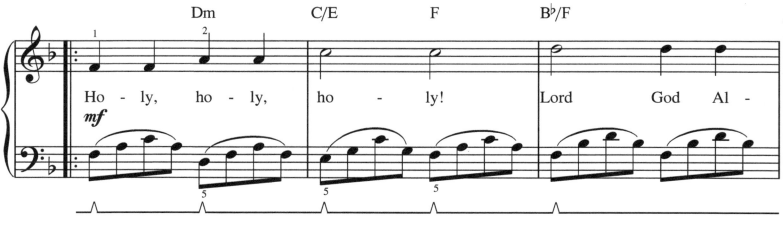

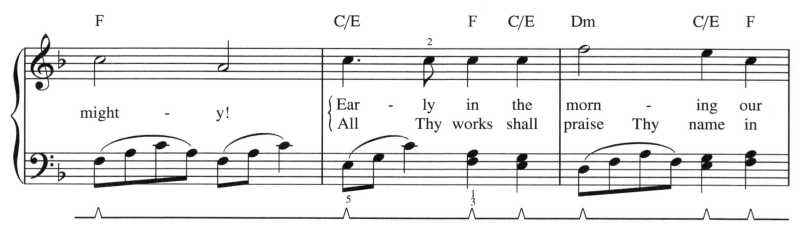

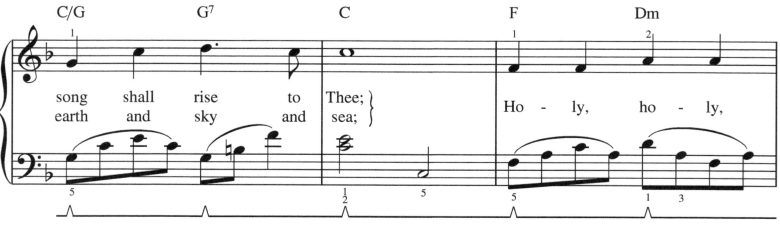

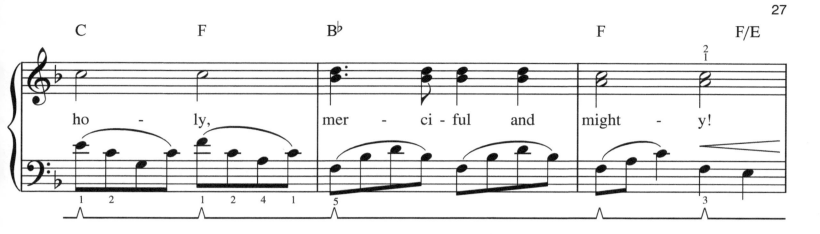

ho - ly, mer - ci - ful and might - y!

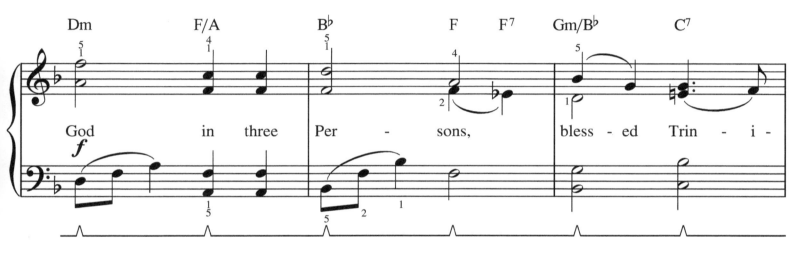

God in three Per - sons, bless - ed Trin - i -

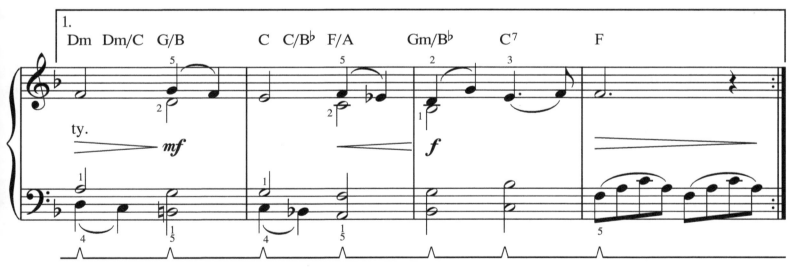

ty.

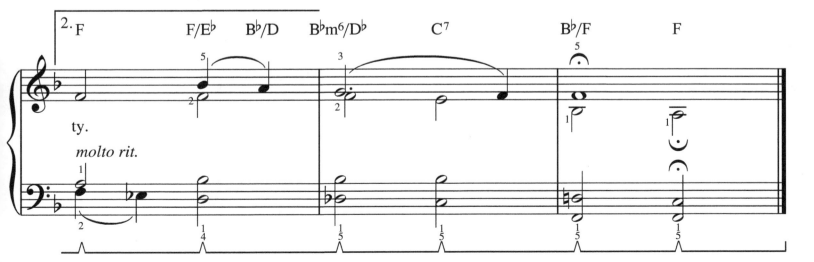

ty.

molto rit.

I SURRENDER ALL

Words by J.W. VAN DEVENTER
Music by W.S. WEEDEN
Arranged by Phillip Keveren

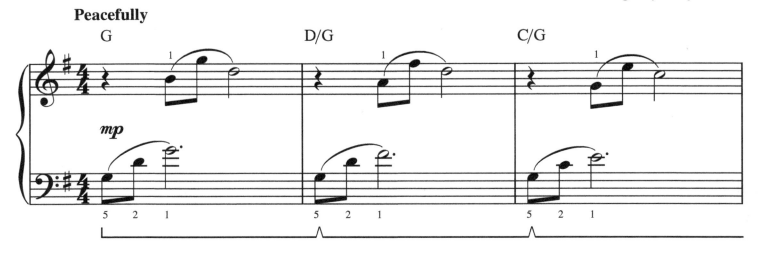

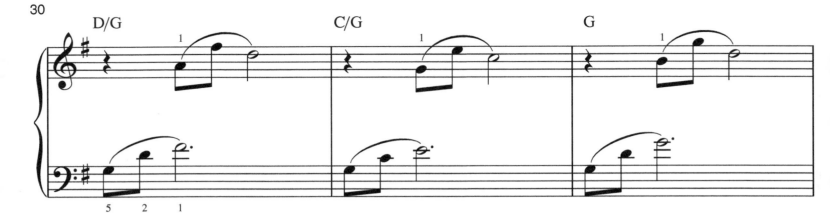
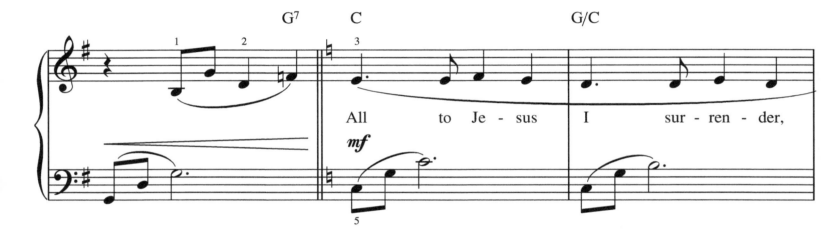
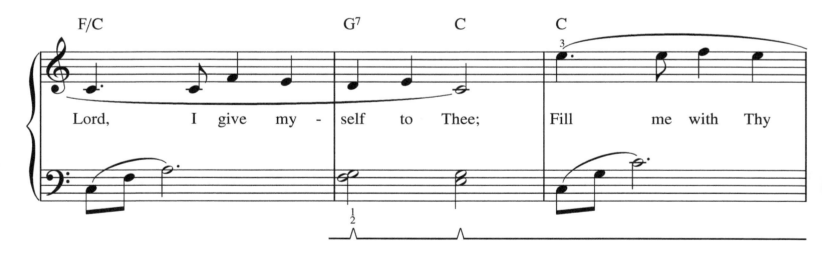

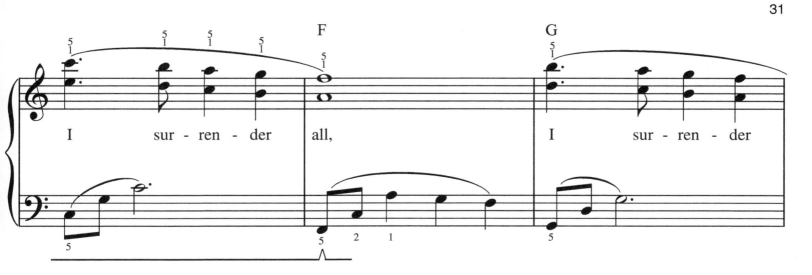

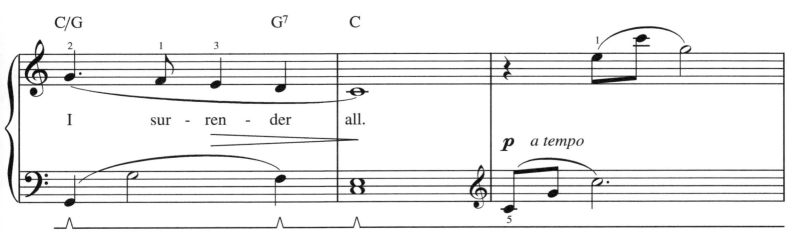

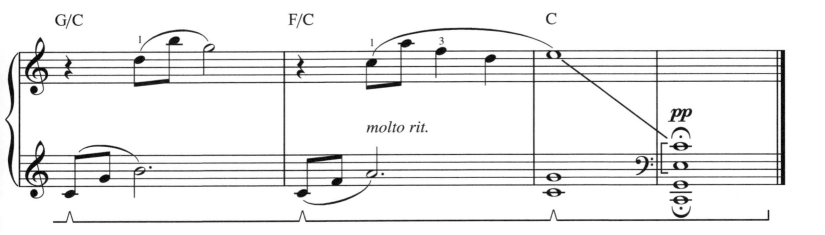

IMMORTAL, INVISIBLE

Words by WALTER CHALMERS SMITH
Traditional Welsh Melody
From John Roberts' *Canaidau y Cyssegr*
Arranged by Phillip Keveren

Triumphantly

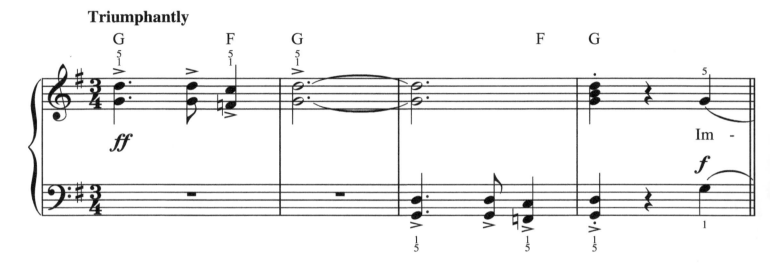

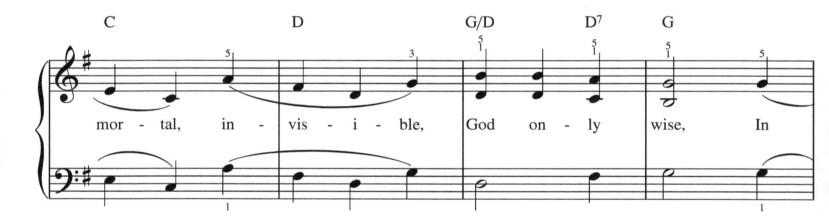

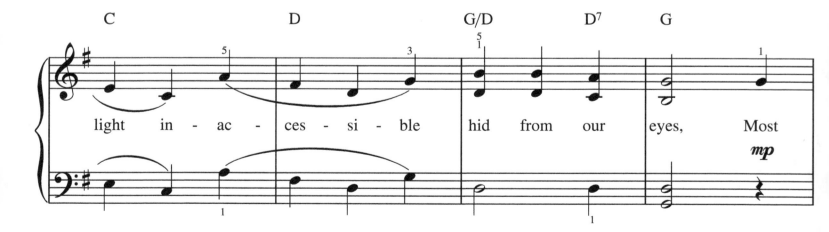

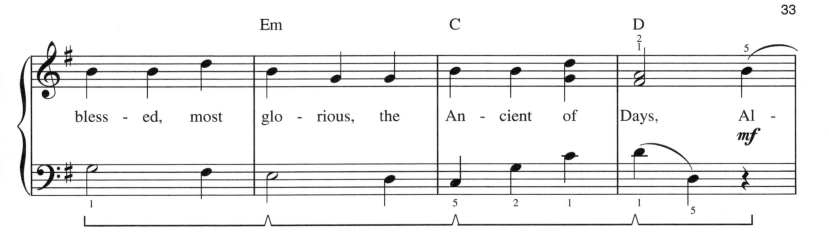

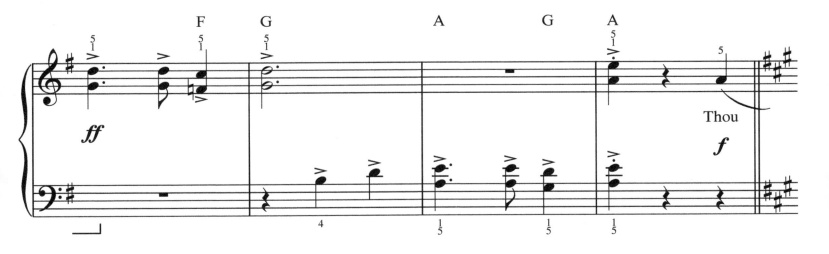

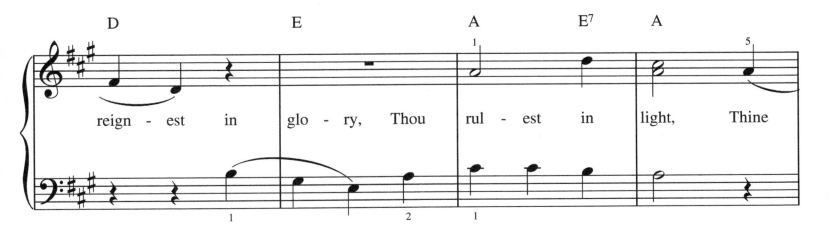

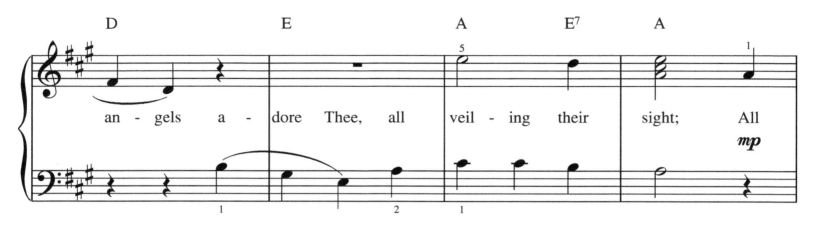

an - gels a - dore Thee, all veil - ing their sight; All

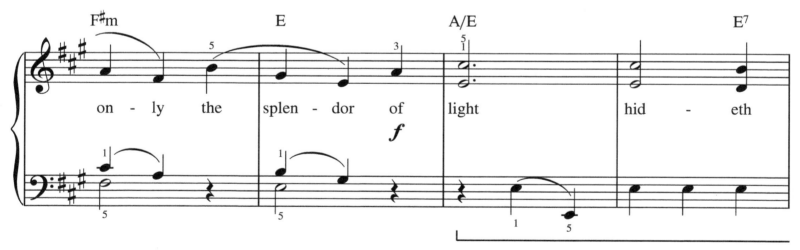

praise we would ren - der; O help us to see 'Tis

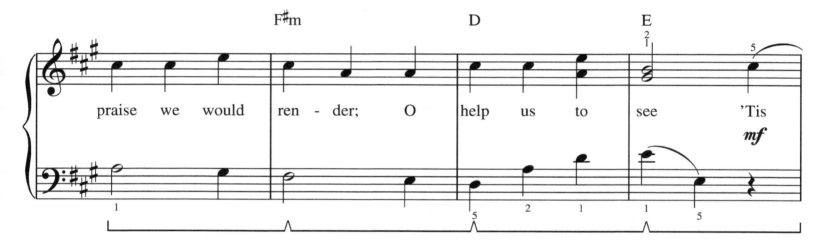

on - ly the splen - dor of light hid - eth

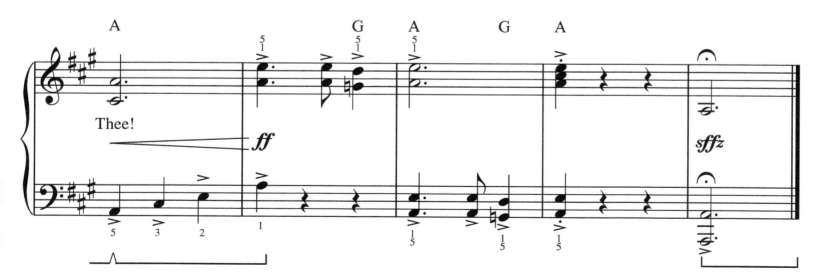

Thee!

IN THE GARDEN

Words and Music by C. AUSTIN MILES
Arranged by Phillip Keveren

Serenely

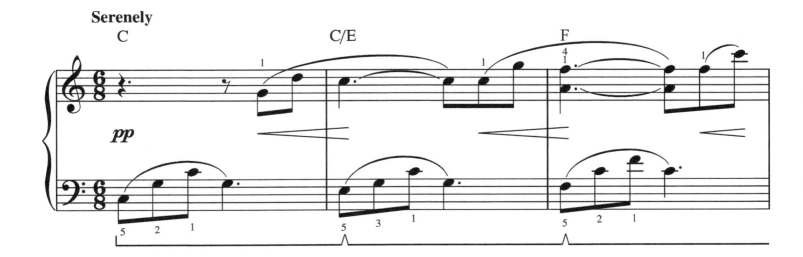

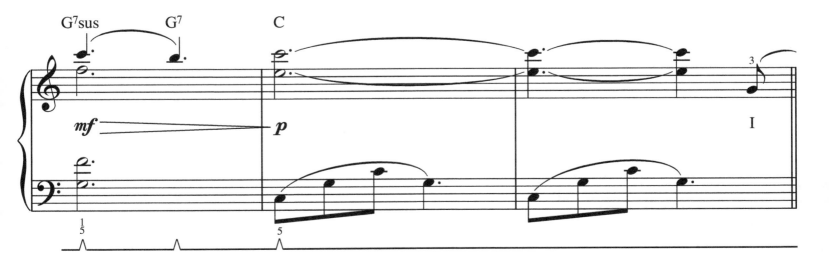

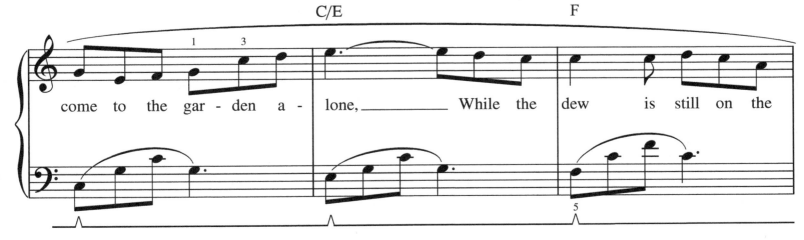

come to the gar - den a - lone,_____ While the dew is still on the

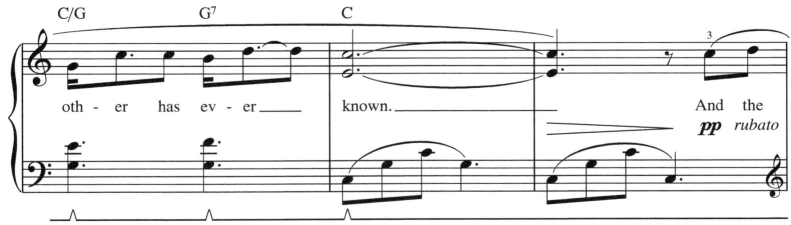

oth - er has ev - er _____ known. _____ And the

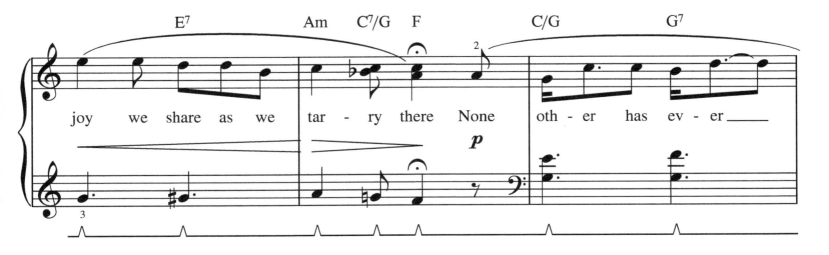

joy we share as we tar - ry there None oth - er has ev - er _____

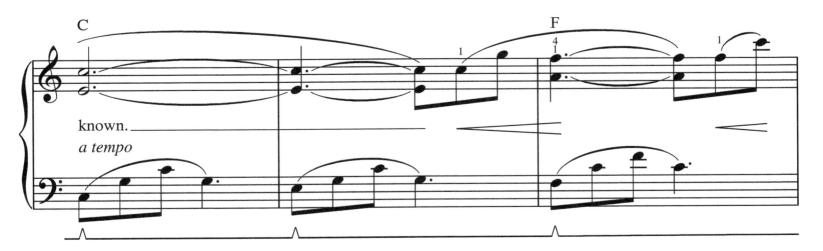

known. _____
a tempo

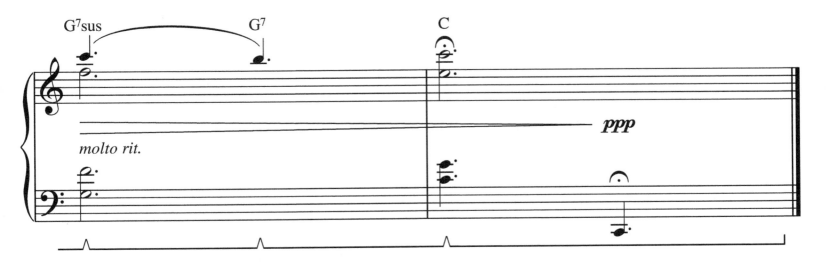

molto rit.

JUST AS I AM

Words by CHARLOTTE ELLIOTT
Music by WILLIAM B. BRADBURY
Arranged by Phillip Keveren

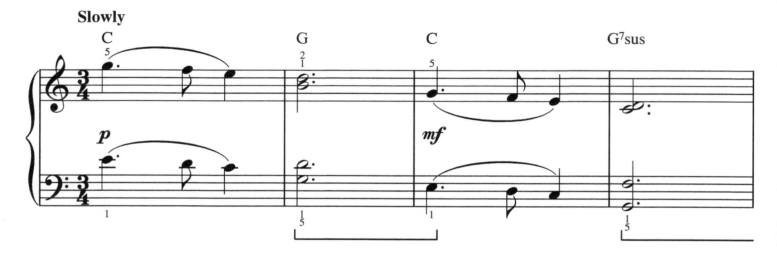

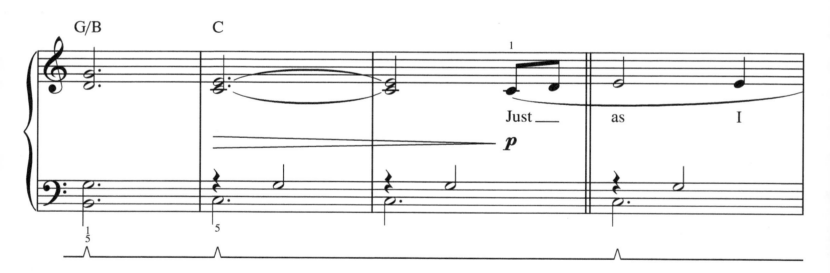

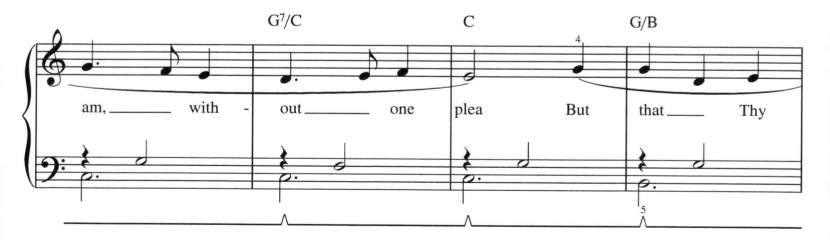

blood was shed for me, And ___ that Thou

bidd'st ___ me come to Thee, ___ O Lamb of

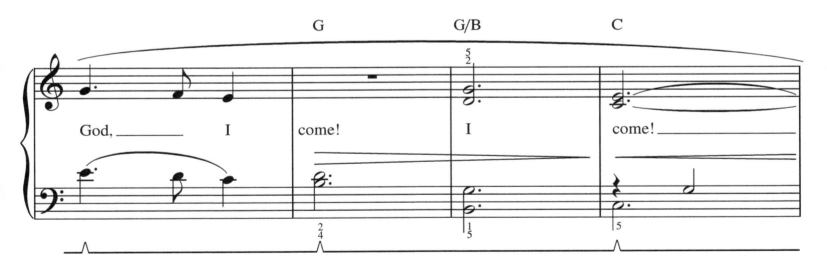

God, ___ I come! I come! ___

Just ___ as I

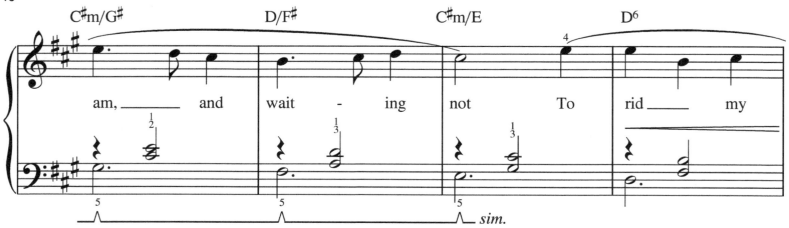

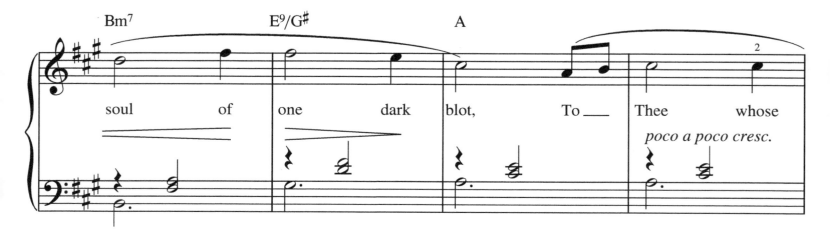

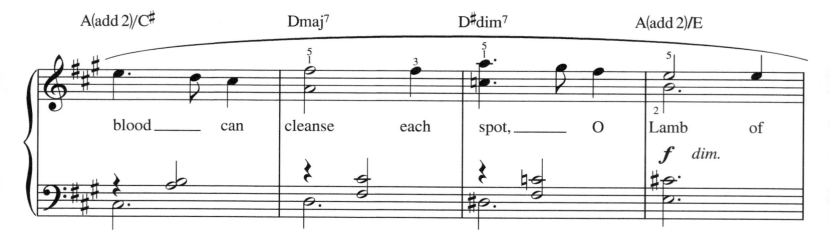

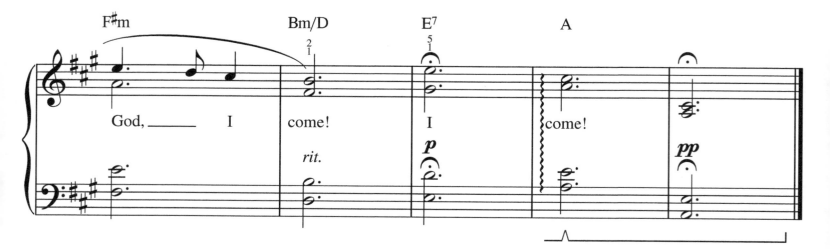

SOFTLY AND TENDERLY

Words and Music by WILL L. THOMPSON
Arranged by Phillip Keveren

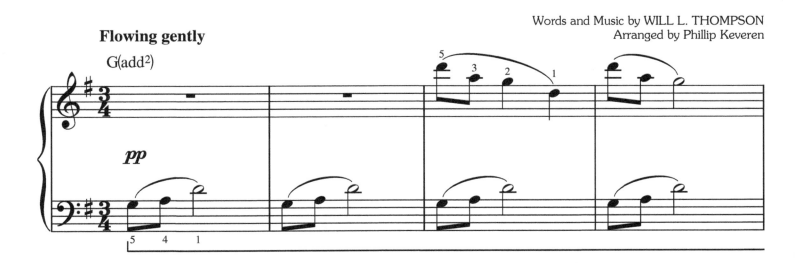

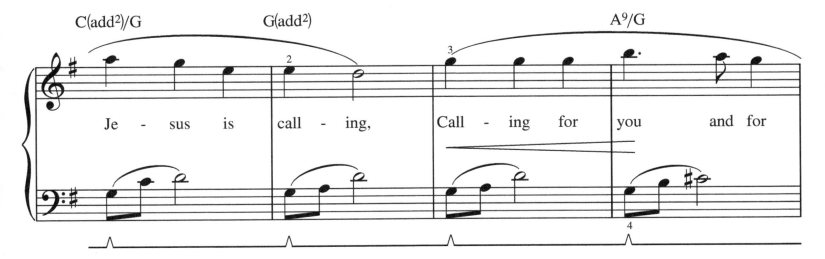

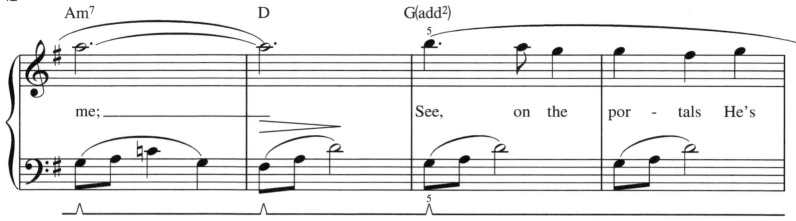

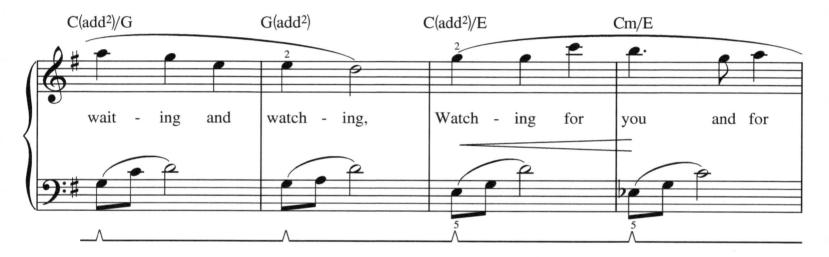

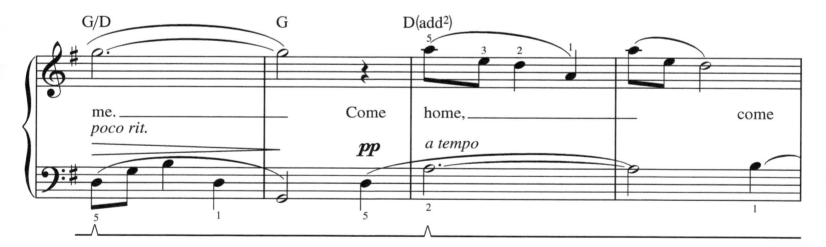

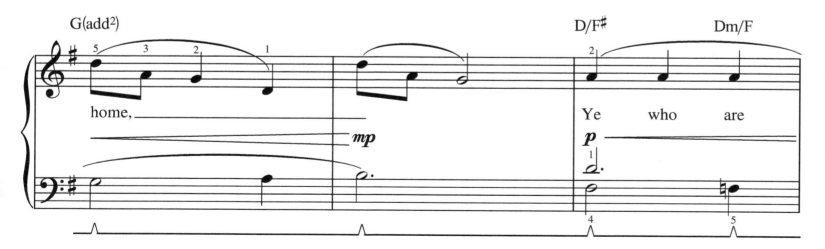

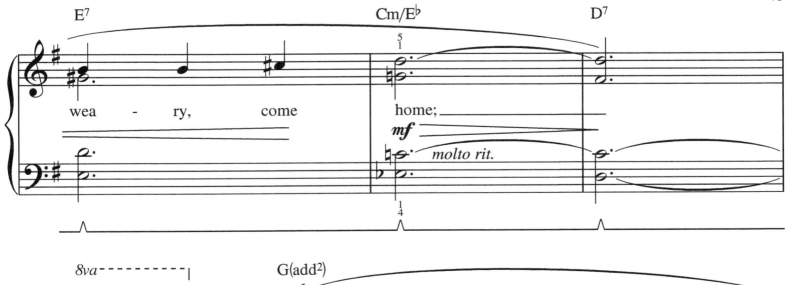

E7   Cm/E♭   D7

wea - ry, come home;

mf

molto rit.

8va

G(add²)

pp

mp   *a tempo*

Ear - nest - ly, ten - der - ly,

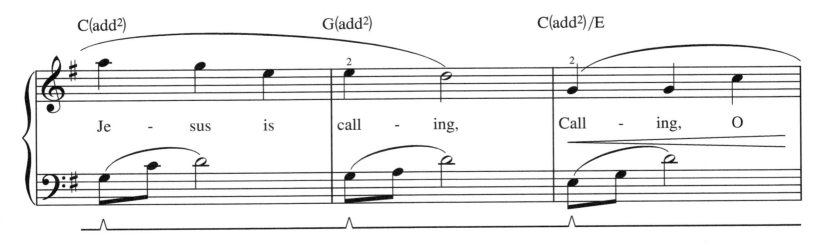

C(add²)   G(add²)   C(add²)/E

Je - sus is call - ing, Call - ing, O

Cm/E♭   G/D   G(add²)

8va

sin - ner, come home!

mf   *dim. e rit.*

pp

LET US BREAK BREAD TOGETHER

Traditional Spiritual
Arranged by Phillip Keveren

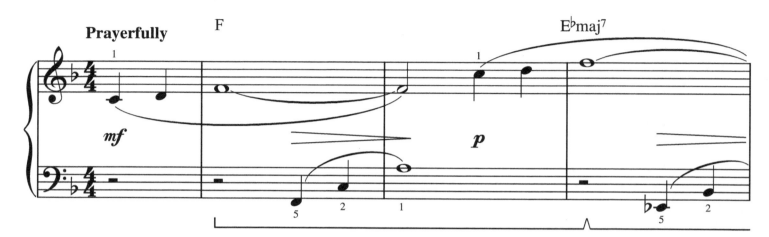

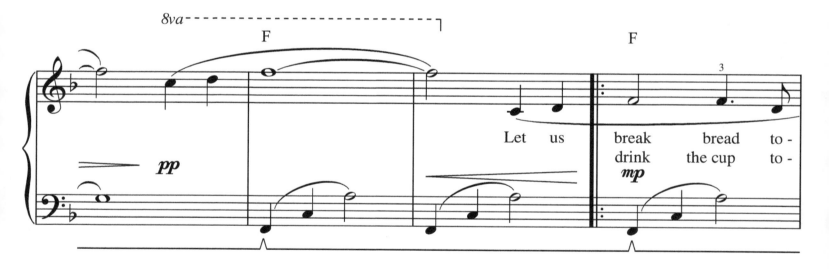

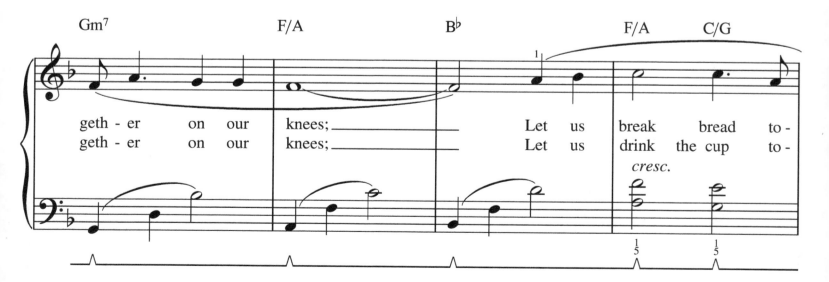

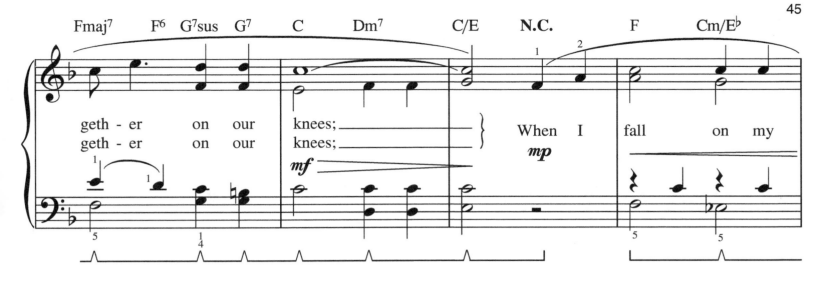

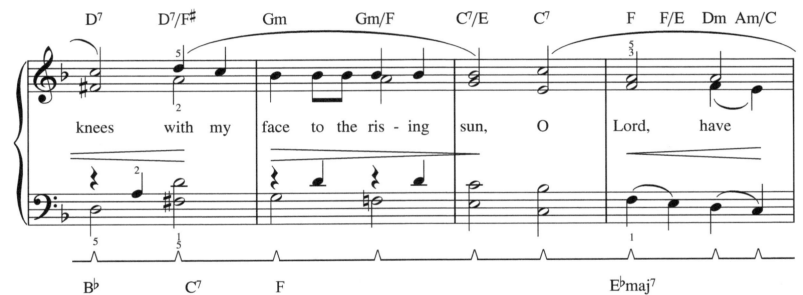

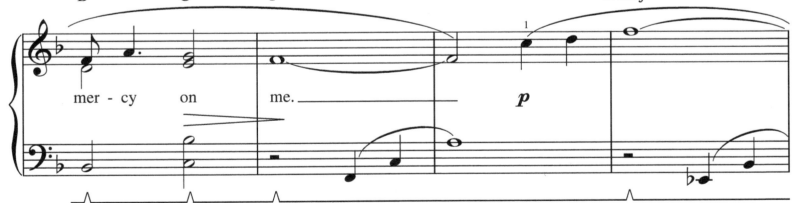

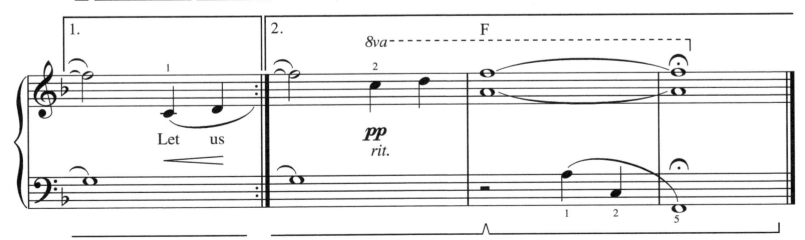

O GOD, OUR HELP IN AGES PAST

Words by ISAAC WATTS
Music by WILLIAM CROFT
Arranged by Phillip Keveren

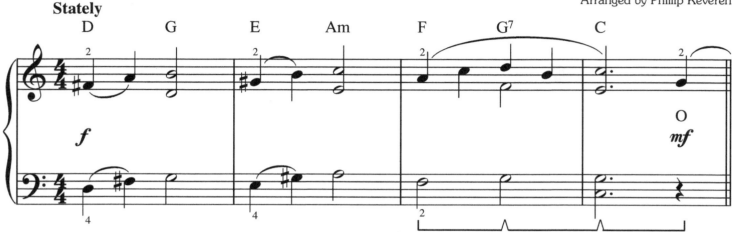

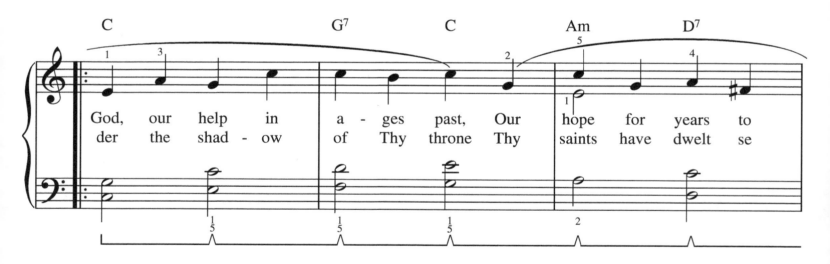

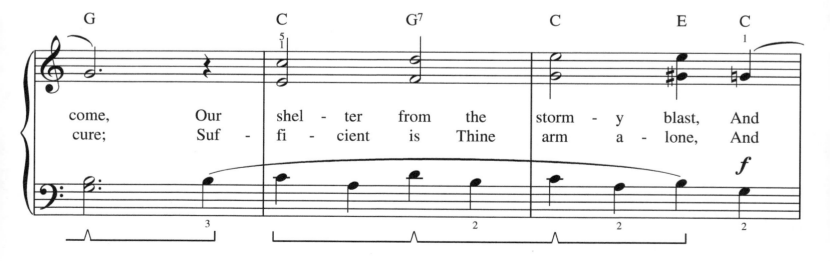

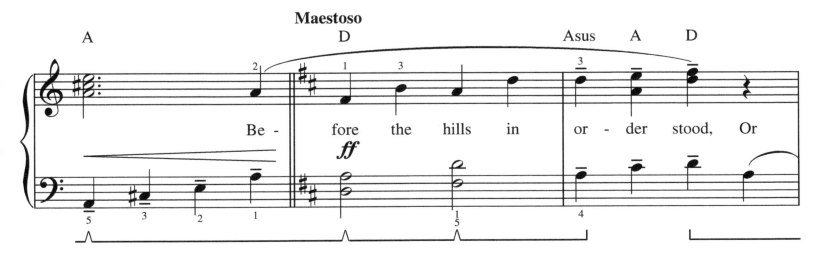

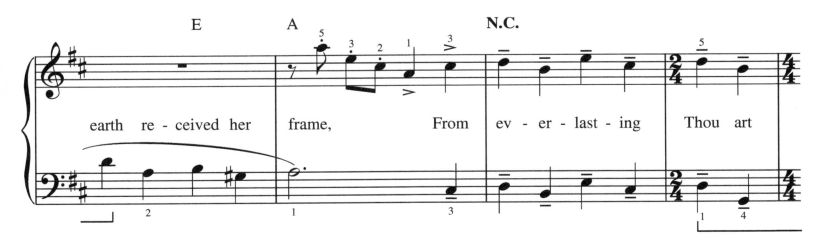

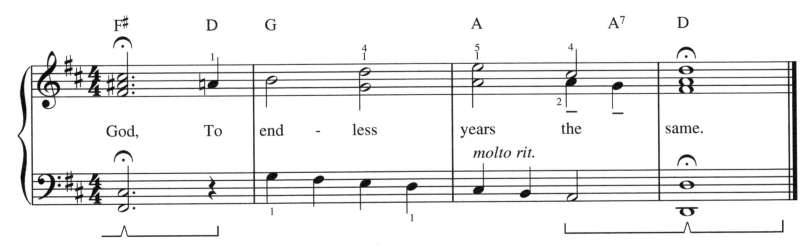

O WORSHIP THE KING

Words by ROBERT GRANT
Based on "Lyons," Attributed to JOHANN MICHAEL HAYDN
Arranged by Phillip Keveren

Majestically, like a brass fanfare

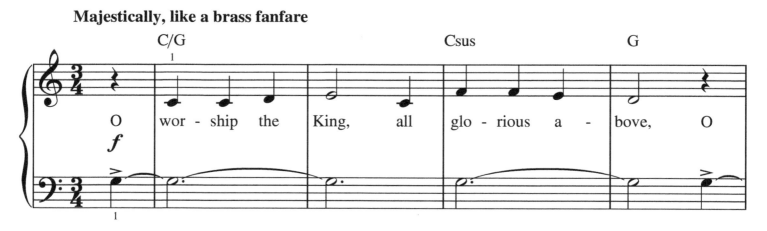

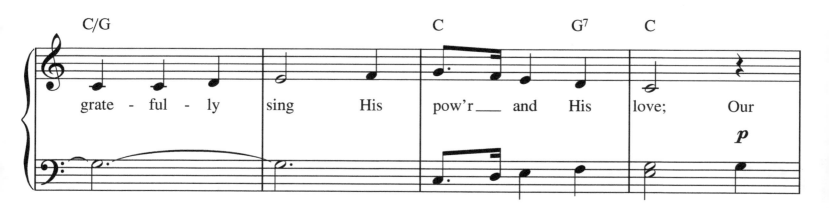

C/G   C   C/G   G⁷   Csus

vil - ioned in   splen - dor, and   gird - ed with   praise.____

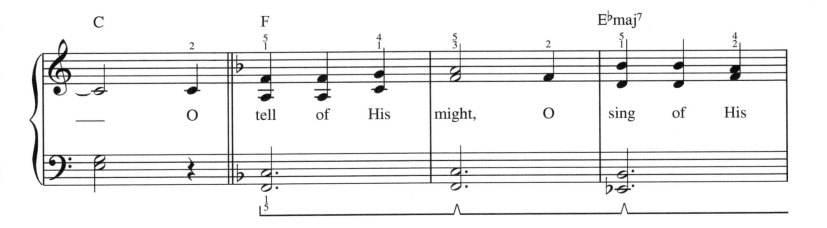

C   F   E♭maj⁷

____ O   tell of His   might, O   sing of His

C   F   F/C   C⁷

grace, Whose   robe is the   light, whose   can - o - py

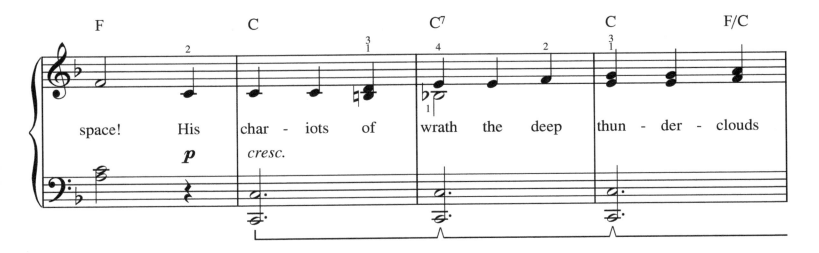

F   C   C⁷   C   F/C

space! His   char - iots of   wrath the deep   thun - der - clouds

p   *cresc.*

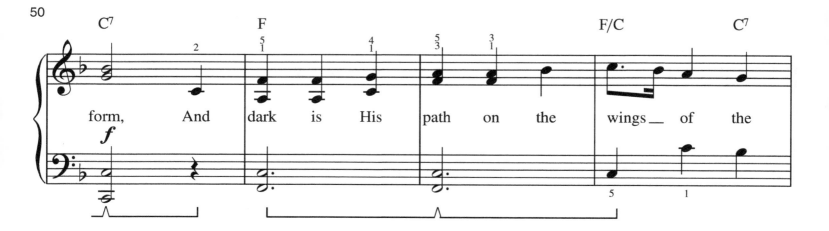

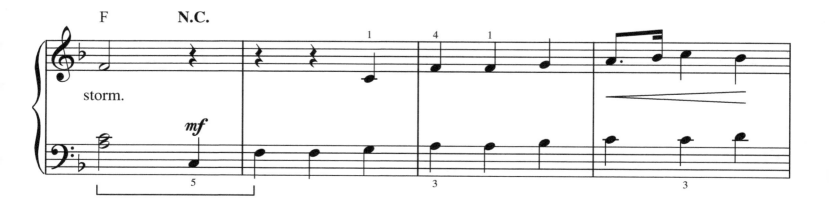

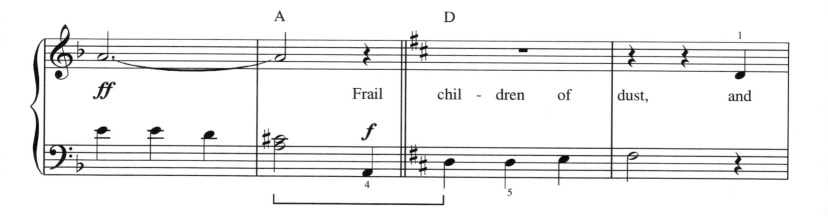

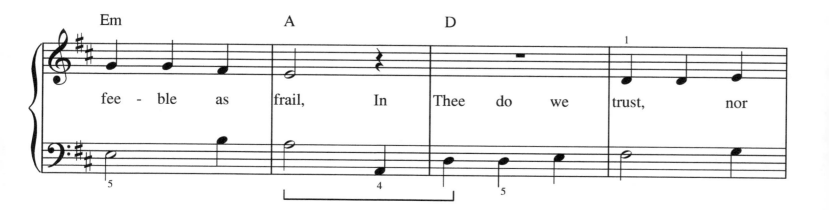

find ___ Thee to fail; Thy mer - cies how ten - der, how

firm to the end, ___ Our Mak - er, De -

Maestoso

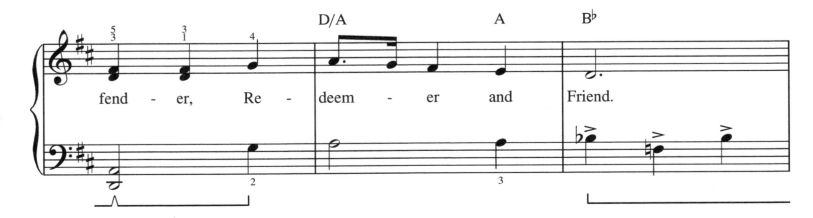

fend - er, Re - deem - er and Friend.

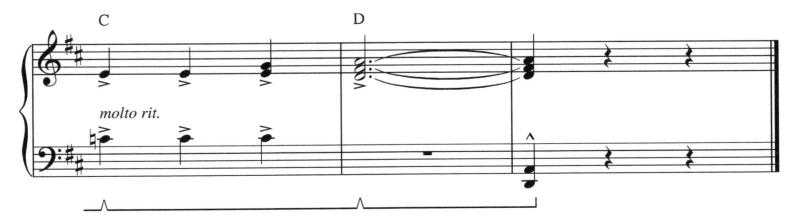

molto rit.

THIS IS MY FATHER'S WORLD

Words by MALTBIE D. BABCOCK
Music by FRANKLIN L. SHEPPARD
Arranged by Phillip Keveren

Peacefully

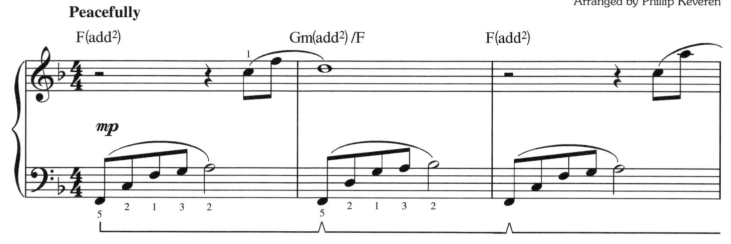

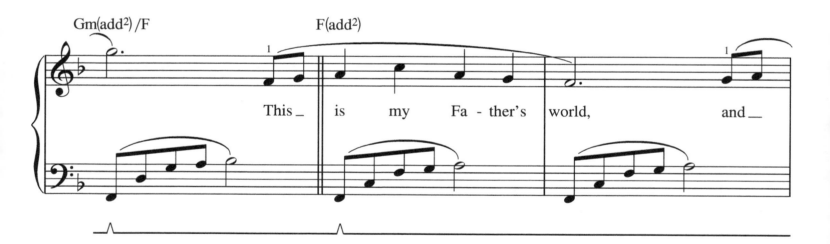

This _ is my Fa - ther's world, and _

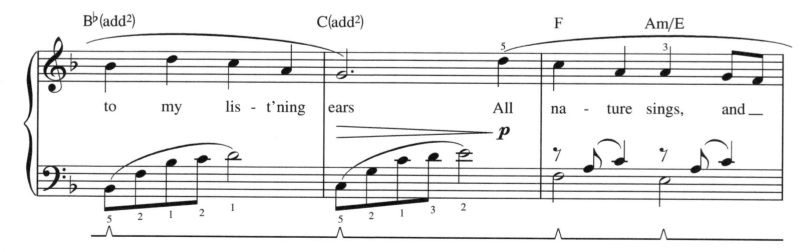

to my lis - t'ning ears All na - ture sings, and _

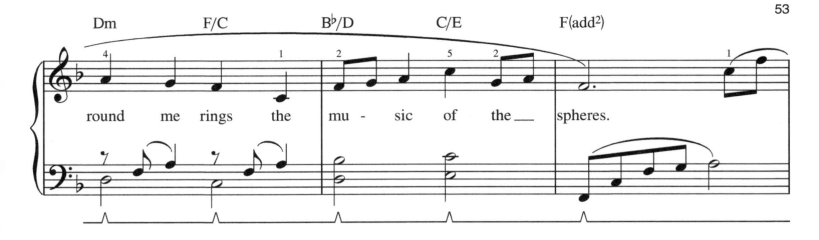

round me rings the mu - sic of the ___ spheres.

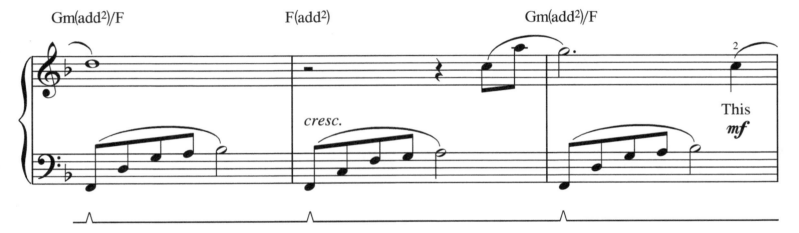

This

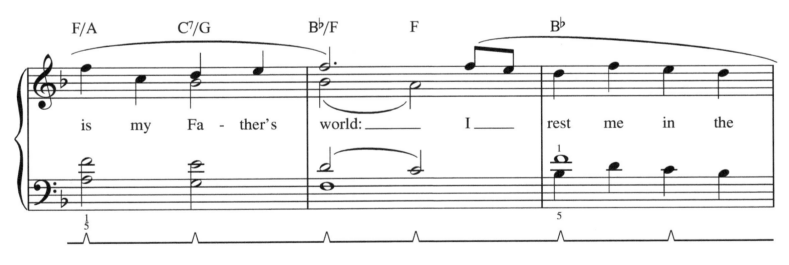

is my Fa - ther's world: ___ I ___ rest me in the

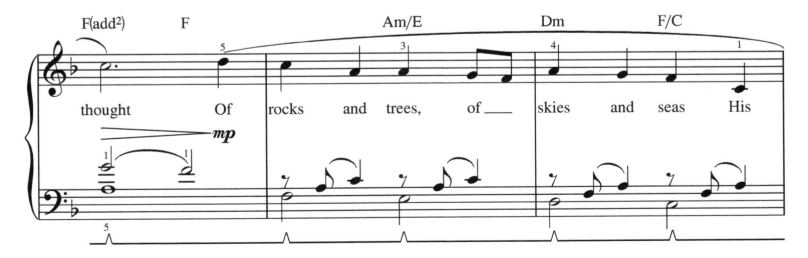

thought Of rocks and trees, of ___ skies and seas His

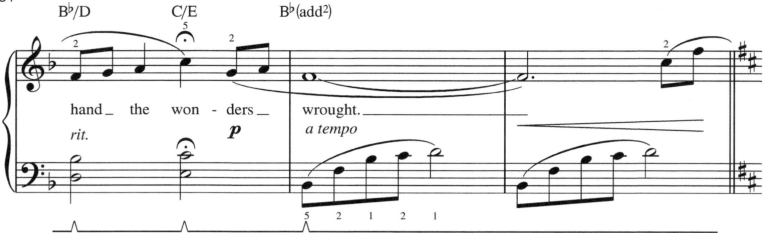

hand __ the won - ders __ wrought. ___
rit.   *p*   *a tempo*

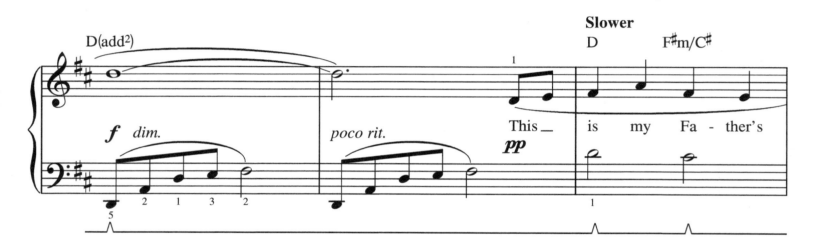

This __ is my Fa - ther's

Slower

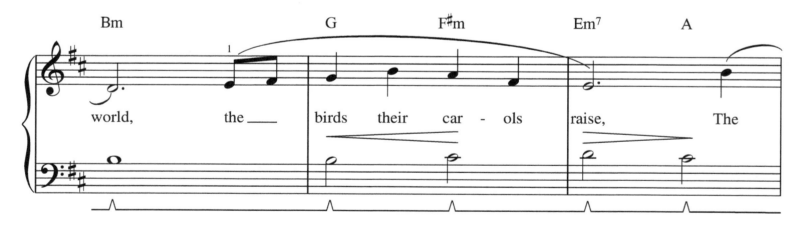

world,   the ___ birds their car - ols raise,   The

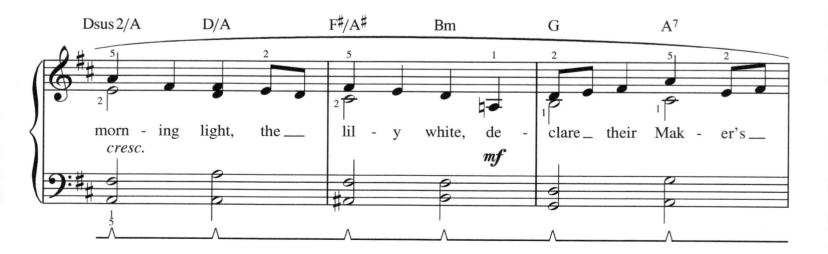

morn - ing light, the ___ lil - y white, de - clare __ their Mak - er's __
cresc.   *mf*

Tempo I

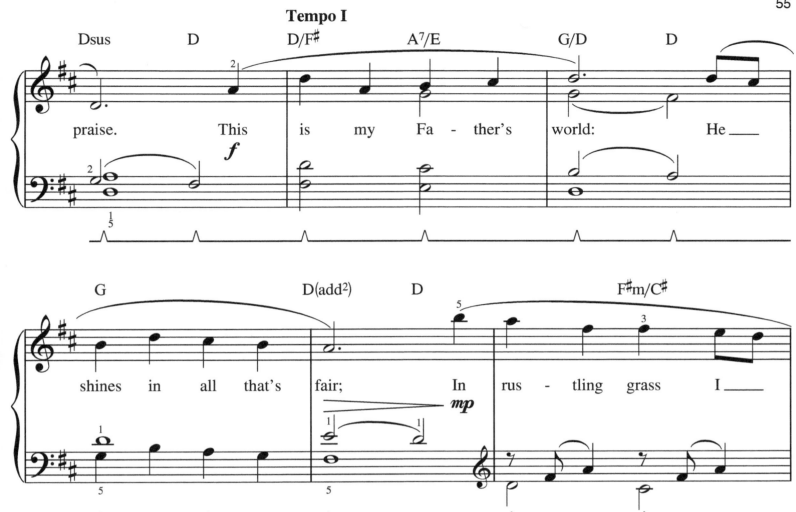

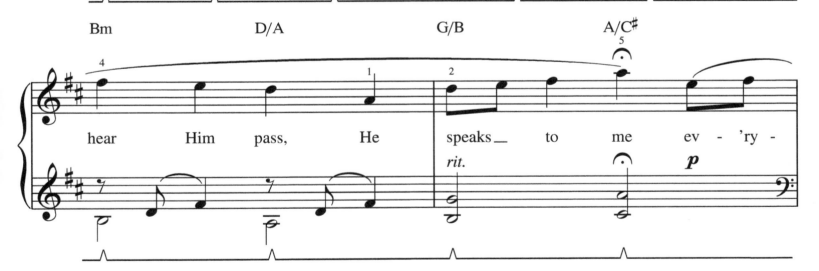

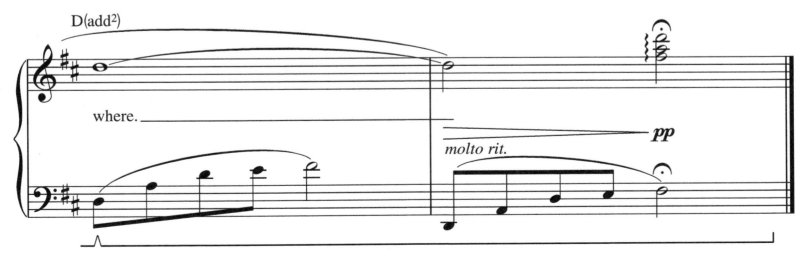

All Hail the Power of Jesus' Name

1. All hail the pow'r of Jesus' name!
   Let angels prostrate fall,
   Let angels prostrate fall;
   Bring forth the royal diadem,
   And crown Him, crown Him, crown Him, crown Him,
   And crown Him Lord of all.

2. Ye chosen seed of Israel's race,
   Ye ransomed from the fall,
   Ye ransomed from the fall;
   Hail Him who saves you by His grace,
   And crown Him, crown Him, crown Him, crown Him,
   And crown Him Lord of all.

3. Sinners, whose love can ne'er forget
   The wormwood and the gall,
   The wormwood and the gall;
   Go spread your trophies at His feet,
   And crown Him, crown Him, crown Him, crown Him,
   And crown Him Lord of all.

4. Let ev'ry kindred, ev'ry tribe,
   On this terrestrial ball,
   On this terrestrial ball;
   To Him all majesty ascribe,
   And crown Him, crown Him, crown Him, crown Him,
   And crown Him Lord of all.

5. Crown Him, ye martyrs of your God,
   Who from His altar call,
   Who from His altar call;
   Extol the Stem of Jesse's Rod,
   And crown Him, crown Him, crown Him, crown Him,
   And crown Him Lord of all.

6. O that with yonder sacred throng
   We at His feet may fall,
   We at His feet may fall!
   We'll join the everlasting song,
   And crown Him, crown Him, crown Him, crown Him,
   And crown Him Lord of all.

And Can It Be That I Should Gain

1. And can it be that I should gain
   An int'rest in the Savior's blood?
   Died He for Me, who caused His pain?
   For me, who Him to death pursued?
   Amazing love! How can it be
   That Thou, my God shouldst die for me?
   Amazing love! How can it be
   That Thou, my God shouldst die for me!

2. He left His Father's throne above,
   So free, so infinite His grace!
   Emptied Himself of all but love,
   And bled for Adam's helpless race!
   'Tis mercy all, immense and free,
   For, O my God, it found out me.
   Amazing love! How can it be
   That Thou, my God, shouldst die for me!

3. Long my imprisoned spirit lay
   Fast bound in sin and nature's night.
   Thine eye diffused a quick'ning ray:
   I woke, the dungeon flamed with light!
   My chains fell off, my heart was free,
   I rose, went forth, and followed Thee.
   Amazing love! How can it be
   That Thou, my God, shouldst die for me!

4. No condemnation now I dread:
   Jesus, and all in Him, is mine!
   Alive in Him my living Head,
   And clothed in righteousness divine,
   Bold I approach th'eternal throne,
   And claim the crown, thee Christ my own.
   Amazing love! How can it be
   That Thou, my God, shouldst die for me!

Be Thou My Vision

1. Be Thou my vision, O Lord of my heart;
   Naught be all else to me, save that Thou art;
   Thou my best thought, by day or by night,
   Waking or sleeping, Thy presence my light.

2. Riches I heed not, nor vain, empty praise.
   Thou mine inheritance, now and always;
   Thou and Thou only, first in my heart,
   Great God of heaven, my treasure Thou art.

3. Be Thou my wisdom, and Thou my true word;
   I ever with Thee and Thou with me, Lord:
   Thou my great Father, I Thy true son,
   Thou in me dwelling, and I with Thee one.

4. High King of heaven, when vict'ry is won,
   May I reach heaven's joys, bright heaven's sun!
   Heart of my heart, whatever befall,
   Still be my vision, O Ruler of all.

Christ the Lord Is Risen Today

1. Christ the Lord is ris'n today, Alleluia!
   Sons of men and angels say: Alleluia!
   Raise your joys and triumphs high, Alleluia!
   Sing, ye heav'ns and earth reply: Alleluia!

2. Love's redeeming work is done, Alleluia!
   Fought the fight, the battle won, Alleluia!
   Death in vain forbids Him rise, Alleluia!
   Christ has opened paradise, Alleluia!

3. Lives again our glorious King, Alleluia!
   Where, O death, is now thy sting? Alleluia!
   Dying once He all doth save, Alleluia!
   Where thy victory, O grave? Alleluia!

4. Soar we now where Christ has led, Alleluia!
   Foll'wing our exalted Head, Alleluia!
   Made like Him, like Him we rise, Alleluia!
   Ours the cross, the grave, the skies, Alleluia!

Come, Thou Almighty King

1. Come, Thou almighty King,
   Help us Thy name to sing, help us to praise:
   Father all glorious, o'er all victorious,
   Come and reign over us, Ancient of Days.

2. Come, Thou incarnate Word,
   Gird on Thy mighty sword, our prayer attend.
   Come and Thy people bless, and give Thy word success,
   Spirit of holiness, on us descend!

3. Come, holy Comforter,
   Thy sacred witness bear in this glad hour.
   Thou, who almighty art, now rule in ev'ry heart,
   And ne'er from us depart, Spirit of pow'r.

4. To Thee, great One in Three,
   Eternal praises be hence evermore!
   Thy sov'reign majesty may we in glory see,
   And to eternity love and adore!

Come, Thou Fount of Every Blessing

1. Come, Thou Fount of ev'ry blessing,
   Tune my heart to sing Thy grace;
   Streams of mercy, never ceasing,
   Call for songs of loudest praise.
   Teach me some melodious sonnet,
   Sung by flaming tongues above;
   Praise His name, I'm fixed upon it,
   Name of God's redeeming love.

2. Here I raise mine Ebenezer;
   Hither by Thy help I'm come;
   And I hope, by Thy good pleasure,
   Safely to arrive at home.
   Jesus sought me when a stranger,
   Wand'ring from the fold of God;
   He, to rescue me from danger,
   Bought me with His precious blood.

3. O to grace how great a debtor
   Daily I'm constrained to be!
   Let Thy goodness, like a fetter,
   Bind my wand'ring heart to Thee.
   Prone to wander, Lord, I feel it,
   Prone to leave the God I love;
   Here's my heart, O take and seal it,
   Seal it for Thy courts above.

God of Our Fathers

1. God of our fathers, whose almighty hand
   Leads forth in beauty all the starry band
   Of shining worlds in splendor through the skies,
   Our grateful songs before Thy throne arise.

2. Thy love divine hath led us in the past,
   In this free land by Thee our lot is cast;
   Be Thou our Ruler, Guardian, Guide and Stay,
   Thy word our law, Thy paths our chosen way.

3. From war's alarms, from deadly pestilence,
   Be Thy strong arm our ever sure defense;
   Thy true religion in our hearts increase,
   Thy bounteous goodness nourish us in peace.

4. Refresh Thy people on their toilsome way,
   Lead us from night to never-ending day;
   Fill all our lives with love and grace divine,
   And glory, laud, and praise be ever Thine.

Holy, Holy, Holy

1. Holy, holy, holy! Lord God Almighty!
   Early in the morning our song shall rise to Thee;
   Holy, holy, holy, merciful and mighty!
   God in three Persons, blessed Trinity!

2. Holy, holy, holy! All the saints adore Thee,
   Casting down their golden crowns around
      the glassy sea;
   Cherubim and seraphim falling down before Thee,
   Which wert and art and evermore shalt be.

3. Holy, holy, holy! Though the darkness hide Thee,
   Though the eye of sinful man Thy glory may not see,
   Only Thou art holy; there is none beside Thee,
   Perfect in pow'r, in love and purity.

4. Holy, holy, holy! Lord God Almighty!
   All Thy works shall praise Thy Name in earth
      and sky and sea;
   Holy, holy, holy, merciful and mighty!
   God in three Persons, blessed Trinity!

I Surrender All

1. All to Jesus I surrender,
   All to Him I freely give;
   I will ever love and trust Him,
   In His presence daily live.
   Refrain:
   I surrender all, I surrender all,
   All to Thee, my blessed Savior,
   I surrender all.

2. All to Jesus I surrender,
   Humbly at His feet I bow;
   Worldly pleasures all forsaken,
   Take me, Jesus, take me now.
   Refrain

3. All to Jesus I surrender,
   Make me, Savior, wholly Thine;
   Let me feel the Holy Spirit,
   Truly know that Thou art mine.
   Refrain

4. All to Jesus I surrender,
   Lord, I give myself to Thee;
   Fill me with Thy love and power,
   Let Thy blessing fall on me.
   Refrain

5. All to Jesus I surrender,
   Now I feel the sacred flame;
   O the joy of full salvation!
   Glory, glory, to His Name!
   Refrain

Immortal, Invisible

1. Immortal, invisible, God only wise,
   In light inaccessible hid from our eyes,
   Most blessed, most glorious, the Ancient of Days,
   Almighty, victorious, Thy great name we praise.

2. Unresting, unhasting, and silent as light,
   Nor wanting, nor wasting, Thou rulest in might;
   Thy justice like mountains high soaring above
   Thy clouds, which are fountains of goodness and love.

3. To all, life Thou givest, to both great and small;
   In all life Thou livest, the true life of all;
   We blossom and flourish like leaves on the tree,
   And wither and perish; but naught changeth Thee.

4. Thou reignest in glory, Thou rulest in light,
   Thine angels adore Thee, all veiling their sight;
   All praise we would render; oh help us to see
   'Tis only the splendor of light hideth Thee!

In the Garden

1. I come to the garden alone,
   While the dew is still on the roses;
   And the voice I hear, falling on my ear,
   The Son of God discloses.
   Refrain:
   And He walks with me and He talks with me,
   And He tells me I am His own;
   And the joy we share as we tarry there
   None other has ever known.

2. He speaks, and the sound of His voice
   Is so sweet the birds stop their singing;
   And the melody that He gave to me
   Within my heart is ringing.
   Refrain

3. I'd stay in the garden with Him,
   Though the night around me be falling;
   But He bids me go; through the voice of woe
   His voice to me is calling.
   Refrain

Just as I Am

1. Just as I am, without one plea
   But that Thy blood was shed for me,
   And that Thou bidd'st me come to Thee,
   O Lamb of God, I come! I come!

2. Just as I am, and waiting not
   To rid my soul of one dark blot,
   To Thee whose blood can cleanse each spot,
   O Lamb of God, I come! I come!

3. Just as I am, though tossed about
   With many a conflict, many a doubt,
   Fightings and fears within, without,
   O Lamb of God, I come! I come!

4. Just as I am, poor, wretched, blind;
   Sight, riches, healing of the mind,
   Yea, all I need in Thee to find,
   O Lamb of God, I come! I come!

5. Just as I am, Thou wilt receive,
   Wilt welcome, pardon, cleanse, relieve;
   Because Thy promise I believe,
   O Lamb of God, I come! I come!

6. Just as I am, Thy love unknown
   Hath broken ev'ry barrier down;
   Now, to be Thine, yes, Thine alone,
   O Lamb of God, I come! I come!

Let Us Break Bread Together

1. Let us break bread together on our knees;
   Let us break bread together on our knees;
   When I fall on my knees with my face to the rising sun,
   O Lord, have mercy on me.

2. Let us drink wine together on our knees;
   Let us drink wine together on our knees;
   When I fall on my knees with my face to the rising sun,
   O Lord, have mercy on me.

3. Let us praise God together on our knees;
   Let us praise God together on our knees;
   When I fall on my knees with my face to the rising sun,
   O Lord, have mercy on me.

O God, Our Help in Ages Past

1. O God, our help in ages past,
   Our hope for years to come,
   Our shelter from the stormy blast,
   And our eternal home:

2. Under the shadow of Thy throne
   Thy saints have dwelt secure;
   Sufficient is Thine arm alone,
   And our defense is sure.

3. Before the hills in order stood,
   Or earth received her frame,
   From everlasting Thou art God,
   To endless years the same.

4. A thousand ages in Thy sight
   Are like an evening gone;
   Short as the watch that ends the night
   Before the rising sun.

5. Time, like an ever rolling stream,
   Bears all our years away;
   They fly, forgotten, as a dream
   Dies at the op'ning day.

6. O God, our help in ages past,
   Our hope for years to come,
   Be Thou our guide while life shall last,
   And our eternal home.

O Worship the King

1. O worship the King, all glorious above,
   O gratefully sing His pow'r and His love;
   Our Shield and Defender, the Ancient of Days,
   Pavilioned in splendor, and girded with praise.

2. O tell of His might, O sing of His grace,
   Whose robe is the light, whose canopy space!
   His chariots of wrath the deep thunderclouds form,
   And dark is His path on the wings of the storm.

3. Thy bountiful care what tongue can recite?
   It breathes in the air, it shines in the light;
   It streams from the hills, it descends to the plain,
   And sweetly distills in the dew and the rain.

4. Frail children of dust, and feeble as frail,
   In Thee do we trust, nor find Thee to fail;
   Thy mercies how tender, how firm to the end,
   Our Maker, Defender, Redeemer and Friend.

Softly and Tenderly

1. Softly and tenderly Jesus is calling,
   Calling for you and for me;
   See, on the portals He's waiting and watching,
   Watching for you and for me.
   Refrain:
   Come home, come home,
   Ye who are weary, come home;
   Earnestly, tenderly, Jesus is calling,
   Calling, O sinner, come home!

2. Why should we tarry when Jesus is pleading,
   Pleading for you and for me?
   Why should we linger and heed not His mercies,
   Mercies for you and for me?
   Refrain

3. Time is now fleeting, the moments are passing,
   Passing from you and from me;
   Shadows are gathering, death's night is coming,
   Coming for you and for me.
   Refrain

4. O, for the wonderful love He has promised,
   Promised for you and for me!
   Though we have sinned, He has mercy and pardon,
   Pardon for you and for me.
   Refrain

This Is My Father's World

1. This is my Father's world, and to my list'ning ears
   All nature sings, and round me rings the music
      of the spheres.

   This is my Father's world: I rest me in the thought
   Of rocks and trees, of skies and seas
   His hand the wonders wrought.

2. This is my Father's world, the birds their carols raise,
   The morning light, the lily white, declare their
      Maker's praise.

   This is my Father's world: He shines in all that's fair;
   In the rustling grass I hear Him pass,
   He speaks to me ev'rywhere.

3. This is my Father's world, O let me ne'er forget
   That though the wrong seems oft so strong,
      God is the Ruler yet.

   This is my Father's world: The battle is not done;
   Jesus who died shall be satisfied,
   And earth and heav'n be one.